BATAAN

BATAAN
A SURVIVOR'S STORY

by **Lt. Gene Boyt**

with **David L. Burch**

Foreword by **Gregory J. W. Urwin**

UNIVERSITY OF OKLAHOMA PRESS • NORMAN

This book is published with the generous assistance of The McCasland Foundation, Duncan, Oklahoma.

Library of Congress Cataloging-in-Publication Data

Boyt, Eugene P., 1917–
    Bataan : a survivor's story / by Gene Boyt with David L. Burch ; foreword by Gregory J.W. Urwin.
        p. cm.
    Includes bibliographical references and index.
    ISBN 0-8061-3582-4 (alk. paper)
        1. Boyt, Eugene P., 1917–   2. World War, 1939–1945—Personal narratives, American.   3. World War, 1939–1945—Prisoners and prisons, Japanese.   4. World War, 1939–1945—Concentration camps—Japan.   5. Bataan, Battle of, Philippines, 1942—Personal narratives.   6. World War, 1939–1945—Atrocities—Philippines.   I. Burch, David L., 1969–   II. Title.

D811.B68946A3 2004
940.54'725991—dc22

2003059500

The paper in this book meets the guidelines for permanence and durability of the Committee on Production Guidelines for Book Longevity of the Council on Library Resources, Inc. ∞

1 2 3 4 5 6 7 8 9 10

*Dedicated with much love, admiration, and thanks
to my wife, Betty Ruth Dietrich Boyt*

GENE BOYT

*In loving memory of my father, Marvin M. Burch, Jr.,
1919–1977, another of the greatest generation's best*

DAVID L. BURCH

CONTENTS

ILLUSTRATIONS

Following page 84

FIGURES

FOREWORD

On January 28, 1944, the *New York Times* jolted drowsy readers out of their Friday-morning routine with an unsettling banner headline: "5,200 AMERICANS, MANY MORE FILIPINOS DIE OF STARVATION, TORTURE AFTER BATAAN." New Yorkers felt their faces flush with anger as they pored over the accompanying front-page report by Lewis Wood:

> Washington, Jan. 27 — Stories of how the Japanese barbarously tortured and cold-bloodedly starved to death and mercilessly murdered more than 5,200 Americans and many times that number of Filipino soldiers captured on Bataan and Corregidor were disclosed in official reports made public jointly by the Army and Navy tonight.
>
> The ghastly recital revealed beatings, allowing parched men to drink only from a carabao wallow, crowding them into barbed-wire bullpens and horsewhipping some who picked up comrades who had collapsed from the terrible heat. . . .[1]

For more than two years, Americans had been inundated by words and images that depicted Japan and its fighting men

---

[1] *New York Times*, 28 January 1944.

as crude, treacherous, and cruel, but this latest informational item did not originate in the imagination of some patriotic copywriter, correspondent, newspaper cartoonist, or Hollywood director.[2] These harrowing tales came from credible eyewitnesses—three American officers who had been captured in the Philippines in April and May 1942—Commander Melvyn H. McCoy of the U.S. Navy, Lieutenant Colonel S. M. Mellnik of the U.S. Army Coast Artillery, and Captain William E. Dyess of the Army Air Forces. On April 4, 1943, they joined seven other American officers in effecting a successful escape from an enemy prison camp on the island of Mindanao. Filipino guerrillas protected and assisted the escapees, and McCoy, Mellnik, and Dyess eventually became the first members of the group to return to the United States.[3]

At various briefings in Australia and America, McCoy, Mellnik, and Dyess stunned their superiors with graphic descriptions of the savage treatment that the Japanese dealt out to helpless prisoners of war (POWs). After one such session, Dyess' superiors remarked: "It is one of the most momentous stories of the war. It is one the American people must know. But do you think they can grasp its enormity? Do you think they can credit it?" President Franklin D. Roosevelt feared that the disclosure of Japanese war crimes would provoke retaliation against American servicemen still in enemy hands, and he initially ordered the suppression of the escapees' revelations. Pressure from General Douglas MacArthur and other

[2] For an astute discussion of the anti-Japanese propaganda that circulated in the United States during World War II, see John W. Dower, *War without Mercy: Race & Power in the Pacific War* (New York: Pantheon Books, 1986).

[3] *New York Times*, 28 January 1944; E. Bartlett Kerr, *Surrender & Survival: The Experience of American POWs in the Pacific 1941-1945* (New York: William Morrow, 1985), 140–44.

sources caused the Roosevelt administration to reverse its position in January 1944, and the sensational story broke in the nation's press before the month's end. To ensure the irrefutability of the testimony offered by McCoy, Mellnik, and Dyess, the War and Navy Departments directed them to avoid any hearsay. They spoke only about what they had seen or experienced, and that turned out to be more than enough to inspire a ferocious backlash against Japan.[4]

Infuriated by the "march of death" that followed Bataan's surrender on April 9, 1942, and a host of additional Japanese atrocities, Americans clamored for revenge. Representative Andrew J. May of Kentucky, the chairman of the House Military Affairs Committee, demanded that his country's fleet set sail immediately "to blow Tokyo off the map." Senator Carl A. Hatch of New Mexico condemned Japanese behavior as a "throwback to barbarism." An editor at the *New York Times* struck a similar note: "The Japanese in war are not men we can understand. They are men of the old Stone Age, animals who sometimes stand erect." These assessments of the enemy help explain why the United States would choose such horrible means as the atomic bomb to end its war with Japan.[5]

The three officers who exposed Japanese outrages in the Philippines did not allow the memory of their testimony to fade with the newsprint on which it originally appeared. Promoted to lieutenant colonel, William Dyess returned to duty as a fighter pilot with the Army Air Forces. Before his prema-

[4] William E. Dyess and Charles Leavelle, *The Dyess Story: The Eye-witness Account of the Death March from Bataan and the Narrative of Experiences in Japanese Prison Camps and of Eventual Escape* (New York: G. P. Putnam's Sons, 1944), 10, 26; Kerr, *Surrender & Survival*, 162-63; *New York Times*, 28 January 1944.

[5] *New York Times*, 29 January 1944; Kerr, *Surrender & Survival*, 163-64; Dower, *War without Mercy*, 51-52.

ture death on December 22, 1943, in a training flight, Dyess dictated a detailed account of his experiences to a reporter from the *Chicago Tribune*. It appeared posthumously in book form in 1944 as *The Dyess Story*. McCoy and Mellnik collaborated on a book of their own, *Ten Escape from Tojo*, which was released that same year.[6]

In the nearly six decades that have passed since World War II, other American survivors of the fall of the Philippines have added to the disturbing record left by McCoy, Mellnik, and Dyess. Some have written memoirs published by commercial, academic, and vanity presses. Others have agreed to be interviewed for museums, archives, their children, and published oral histories. Taken collectively, these preserved memories present a catalog of horrors so monstrous that it still has the power to elicit intense emotional reactions. The fact that the Japanese people have chosen to shield themselves from this shameful chapter in their history with a government-sponsored program of collective amnesia has left American veterans of the 1941-42 Philippine campaign seething with resentment. Japan's stubborn adherence to mass denial makes it imperative that every Allied ex-prisoner of the Pacific Theater who is willing to relive his or her nightmares receives a hearing.[7]

[6] Dyess and Leavelle, *Dyess Story*, 11-20. See also Melvyn H. McCoy and S. M. Mellnik, *Ten Escape from Tojo* (New York: Farrar & Rinehart, Inc., 1944).

[7] In 1990, several former POWs and civilian internees from the Pacific Theater founded the Center for Internee Rights, Inc. (CFIR), to seek an apology and compensation from the Japanese government for the mistreatment of captured Allied military personnel and civilians during World War II. The organization's ongoing crusade and the continued indifference of Japanese officials may be monitored on the CFIR web site at *http://www.expows.com/home_page.htm*. The attitude of the former POWs is also well expressed in Linda Goetz Holmes, *Unjust Enrichment: How Japan's Companies Built Postwar Fortunes Using American POWs* (Mechanicsburg: Stackpole Books, 2001).

With the publication of *Bataan: A Survivor's Story*, Eugene P. Boyt becomes the latest and possibly one of the last voices to join the mournful chorus that bears witness to the physical and mental tortures that the Japanese military inflicted on American troops captured in the Philippines. Like the memoirs penned by Boyt's comrades, this book is not suitable fare for the squeamish. It offers intimate encounters with death, misery, and degradation. For Boyt, World War II not only meant danger and uncertainty but also abject suffering—more than three years of starvation, deprivation, humiliation, and disease.

By all rights, this should be a bitter book. When the U.S. Army assigned Second Lieutenant Boyt to the Philippine Department in early July 1941, it selected him for what military men in an earlier age called a "forlorn hope." The American eagle, with its characteristic indifference to long-range consequences, fastened its talons on the Philippine Islands at the dawn of the twentieth century. Almost as soon as American armed forces quelled native resistance, military planners in Washington realized the impossibility of retaining the archipelago in the event of war with Japan. The Philippines sat 5,500 miles farther from the United States than Japan, and the American government was not prepared to furnish a land garrison and naval support powerful enough to safeguard such a large area so far from home. The disarmament policies that Washington embraced after World War I further undermined the American position in East Asia. Even the most optimistic strategists asked the archipelago's defenders to do nothing more than deny the invading Japanese access to Manila Bay by holding Corregidor and the Bataan peninsula until the U.S. Fleet could steam to the rescue. Then in the early months of 1941, the United States redefined its military priorities by identifying Germany as a graver threat than Japan. A future war would see the bulk of America's military forces committed to Germany's early defeat. That meant America would respond to hostilities in the Pacific by conducting a strategic defense along the Alaska-Hawaii-Panama triangle. In other words, the Philippines had been written off, and that decision made Lieutenant Boyt and the rest of the archipelago's token garrison pawns to be sacrificed for the appearance of national honor.[8]

Just a few weeks after Boyt received his orders to ship out for Manila, the War Department executed an abrupt about-face with its Pacific strategy. On July 31, 1941, General George C. Marshall, the U.S. Army's chief of staff, stunned his subordinates by announcing "it was [now] the policy of the United States to defend the Philippines." America's altered posture rested on a misplaced faith in technology and the expectation that Japan would strike later rather than sooner. The U.S. Army Air Forces proposed deterring Japanese aggression in East Asia by stationing 330 heavy bombers and 260 fighters in the Philippines. American airmen boasted that their B-17 "Flying Fortresses" could burn Japan's cities to the ground and close enemy sea lanes upon the opening of hostilities. One hundred and sixty-five newly produced bombers would be ready for delivery to the Philippines by the end of February 1942. In the meantime, the War Department began sending land reinforcements to the archipelago, and Lieutenant General Douglas MacArthur strove to complete the mobilization of the ten reserve divisions belonging to the Philippine Army by mid-December 1941. General Marshall explained, "If

[8] Louis Morton, *Strategy and Command: The First Two Years*, The United States Army in World War II: The War in the Pacific, part 15, edited by Stetson Conn (Washington, D.C.: Office of the Chief of Military History, Department of the Army, 1962), 22-23, 25-42, 81-91; Samuel Eliot Morison, *History of United States Naval Operations in World War II*, Vol. 3: *The Rising Sun in the Pacific, 1931-April 1942* (Boston: Little, Brown, 1948), 51-52.

we could make the Philippines reasonably defensible, particularly with heavy bombers, . . . we felt we could block the Japanese advance and block their entry into war by fear of what would happen if they couldn't take the Philippines."[9] Time ran out before the U.S. Army could shift enough of its strength to the Philippines to make a difference in determining the archipelago's future. As of July 26, 1941, there were 10,560 American troops on duty in the Philippine Department. That figure grew to only 19,116 officers and men by November 30.

Fewer than three dozen B-17s were available to MacArthur at the outbreak of war a week later, and he would soon learn that the Flying Fortress was not the invulnerable wonder weapon his superiors assumed it to be. Most of the 100,000 men who composed the Philippine Army were poorly trained, poorly armed, and under-equipped draftees, although the 12,000 Filipino Scouts who made up an integral part of the U.S. Army were as good as any American regulars. Incredibly, MacArthur thought he could take this hastily assembled and unfinished force and conduct a mobile defense that would deny the Japanese a foothold on Luzon, the archipelago's main island.[10]

[9] Russell F. Weigley, "The Role of the War Department and the Army," in *Pearl Harbor as History: Japanese-American Relations*, eds. Dorothy Borg and Shumpei Okamoto (New York: Columbia University Press, 1973), 182-83; Wesley Frank Craven and James Lea Cate, eds., *The Army Air Forces in World War II*, Vol. 1: *Plans and Early Operations, January 1939 to August 1942* (Chicago: University of Chicago Press, 1948), 17, 53, 172, 178-79, 182; Marshall quoted in Forrest C. Pogue, *George C. Marshall: Ordeal and Hope, January 1939-1942* (New York: Viking Press, 1966), 193; Louis Morton, *The Fall of the Philippines*. The United States Army in World War II: The War in the Pacific, part 4, edited by Kent Roberts Greenfield (Washington, D.C.: Office of the Chief of Military History, Department of the Army, 1953), 37-38; Daniel F. Harrington, "A Careless Hope: American Air Power and Japan, 1941," *Pacific Historical Review* 48 (May 1979): 225-26; Morton, *Strategy and Command*, 98.

[10] Morton, *Fall of the Philippines*, 21, 25-27, 37-45, 48-50.

General MacArthur's blind hubris and America's inadequate war preparations doomed Gene Boyt and his comrades on Luzon. *Bataan: A Survivor's Story* presents a vivid portrait of that desperate campaign. Readers will taste some of the terror of being exposed to Japanese air raids, the anxiety of a hectic retreat, and the numbing strain of more than three months of combat while subsisting on starvation rations during the siege of Bataan. Boyt's reminiscences are unique among those chronicling this phase of the Pacific War because they illuminate the work of MacArthur's engineers. Surrender should have freed Boyt and Bataan's other gaunt defenders from the fear of violent death, but they were denied that mercy. Captivity hurled them into unimaginable torments.[11]

The Japanese forces that conquered the Philippines were neither prepared nor disposed to provide proper care for large numbers of prisoners of war. Consequently, more than 40 percent of the American servicemen who escaped death in combat during the defense of the Philippines would not live to see home again. Of the 25,580 American soldiers, sailors, and Marines who surrendered in the Philippines in the spring of 1942, 10,650 perished in enemy hands. Most of these men died slow, agonizing deaths from complications brought on by malnutrition, dehydration, disease, and physical abuse. At any time, the Japanese proved capable of executing prisoners on the slightest pretext. Finally, too many POWs died from American bombing or torpedoing of the unmarked ships their cap-

---

[11] Ronald H. Spector offers a particularly scathing critique of MacArthur's generalship in *Eagle against the Sun: The American War with Japan* (New York: Free Press, 1985), 72-74, 106-19. See also Williamson Murray and Allan R. Millett, *A War to Be Won: Fighting the Second World War* (Cambridge: Belknap Press of Harvard University Press, 2000), 181-85. The best overview of the trials endured by Boyt and his fellow POWs is Gavan Daws, *Prisoners of the Japanese: POWs of World War II in the Pacific* (New York: William Morrow, 1994).

tors employed to transport them to the Japanese home islands in the latter part of the war. Raised in an era when Caucasians automatically assumed that they were superior to people of color, these Americans lived for three-and-a-half years at the mercy of Asians who openly despised them as a race of selfish individualists and dishonorable cowards. The trauma these POWs endured was psychological as well as physical.[12]

It should come as no surprise that the survivors of Bataan and Corregidor are haunted by demons that have yet to be exorcised despite sixty years of physical freedom. Who could forget the pitiful sights that Major Alva R. Fitch, an artilleryman captured on Bataan, witnessed at Camp O'Donnell in April and May 1942? "I have seen men," Fitch wrote, "try to go from barracks to the latrine who were too weak and would fall down in the mud and rain, unable to rise—their friends, officers or enlisted men, would sit in the barracks sheltered from the rain and look at them without moving to help them. I have seen men, not one but fifty or more at a time, lying in their own feces too weak to move and no one to move them."[13]

Driven to the brink of despair by their Japanese captors,

[12] Charles A. Stenger, *American Prisoners of War in WWI, WWII, Korea and Vietnam: Statistical Data Concerning Numbers Captured, Repatriated and Still Alive* (Washington, D.C.: Veterans Administration Advisory Committee on Former POWs, 1 January 1981), 3-4; Stanley G. Sommers, ed., *The Japanese Story* (Marshfield, Wis.: American Ex-Prisoners of War, 1980), D, 13-14, 46, 80; Stanley L. Falk, *Bataan: The March of Death* (New York: Norton, 1962), 194-99, 226-27; Donald Knox, *Death March: The Survivors of Bataan* (New York: Harcourt Brace Jovanovich, 1981), xi, 155, 157; D. Clayton James, ed., *South to Bataan, North to Mukden: The Prison Diary of Brigadier General W. E. Brougher* (Athens: University of Georgia Press, 1971), 41-42. See also Gregory F. Michno, *Death on the Hellships: Prisoners at Sea in the Pacific War* (Annapolis: Naval Institute Press, 2001).

[13] Alva R. Fitch, "The Siege of Bataan from the Bottom of a Foxhole," 22 April 1943, 31, in Alva R. Fitch Papers, U.S. Army Military History Institute, Carlisle Barracks; Knox, *Death March*, xiii.

many of the Americans surrounding Boyt became predators. Reflecting on life in the prison camp at Cabanatuan, Second Lieutenant Charles W. Burris, a fighter pilot, arrived at this disillusioned conclusion: "That was one place where I learned that a human being is a marauder. I believe he would steal from his own mother if he was starving hard enough. You couldn't keep food around because they'd steal it. . . . They [the POWs] didn't mind seeing a guy die. They just wanted the food. Everybody was concerned about themselves." The ragged and hungry army that had inspired the free world with its dogged stands on Bataan and Corregidor lost its spirit and crumbled during the early weeks of confinement. "Discipline generally collapsed at the time of surrender," explained First Lieutenant Jack Hawkins of the Fourth Marines, MacArthur's sole U.S. Marine regiment. "Many of the men would no longer obey the orders of their officers. Many of the officers on the other hand, abandoned all responsibility and made no effort to control or take care of the men."[14]

Eventually, POW officers stopped feeling sorry for themselves and reimposed the discipline and order necessary to keep their remaining men from destroying one another. Nevertheless, no one could put a complete stop to the victimization of the prisoners by the gamblers and black marketers among them. It is no wonder that many of Bataan's "battling bastards" emerged from captivity with a jaundiced view of life. Most have attempted to conceal their cynicism by declining to talk about the war, but those who break their silence cannot always resist the temptation to blurt out the hard lessons

[14] Robert S. LaForte, Ronald E. Marcello, and Richard L. Himmel, eds., *With Only the Will to Live: Accounts of Americans in Japanese Prison Camps, 1941-1945* (Wilmington, Del.: SR Books, 1994), 61-62, 64, Burris quoted on 62; Knox, *Death March*, 135-36, 158-59, 166, 203, 207, 251, 265; Jack Hawkins, *Never Say Die* (Philadelphia: Dorrance & Company, 1961), 72-76.

they learned in prison camp. When Corporal W. Pat Hitchcock of the Fourth Marines published his POW memoir, *Forty Months in Hell*, in 1996, he made no apologies for including this diary entry that he scribbled at Cabanatuan: "If I leave this prison camp with any illusions of man's kindness to fellowman or belief in the Golden Rule as a standard rather than hackneyed sentimentalism, I pray someone boots my can up to my shoulders. It's dog eat dog and the only consideration shown your friends is you don't hook them. And keep your fingers crossed that they reciprocate." Captain Marion Lawton, a Death March survivor from the Thirty-first U.S. Infantry Regiment, ended up thinking like Hitchcock after an acquaintance refused to loan him a little money to purchase black market food at Cabanatuan. "This thing is survival, every man for himself," Lawton realized. "If he gives me what he has, then he's going to have problems. It taught me a lesson. You shouldn't expect anything out of a casual relationship. It's only within a family that people can turn to each other for real help." These bleak sentiments are not the reassuring message that Americans have come to expect from the generation that weathered World War II, but they remind us of the terrible scars, psychological as well as physical, this titanic conflict left on the millions of lives it affected.[15]

Fortunately, readers desiring a nobler vision of the human species will find it in Gene Boyt's *Bataan: A Survivor's Story*. This is not a diatribe from a man with scores to settle. While

---

[15] John R. Bumgarner, *Parade of the Dead: A U.S. Army Physician's Memoir of Imprisonment by the Japanese, 1942-1945* (Jefferson, N. C.: McFarland & Company, 1995), ix.; Michno, *Death on the Hellships*, vii; W. Pat Hitchcock, *Forty Months in Hell* (Jackson, Tennessee: Page Publishing, 1996), 78-79. Lawton quoted in Knox, *Death March*, 215. See also Guy J. Kelnhofer, *Understanding the Former Prisoner of War: Life after Liberation* (St. Paul, Minnesota: Banfil Street Press, 1992).

Boyt pulls no punches in describing Japanese brutality and the misbehavior of his fellow prisoners, he does not fixate on the evils that he witnessed. Boyt also highlights the courage, kindness, and ingenuity exhibited by those POWs whose struggle for survival did not lead them into forsaking their comrades—the brother engineer officers who took Boyt into their barracks at Camp O'Donnell, the authoritarian major who enforced discipline at Camp Tanaguaw and constantly badgered the Japanese to improve his men's living conditions, and the doctor with no medicines who preserved his patients' will to live and demonstrated the power of positive thinking by prescribing placebos.[16]

Gene Boyt's hellish experiences failed to persuade him that human beings are devils. As he states up front in his introduction: "Bataan has not extinguished my faith in humanity. I still believe that most people, regardless of their race, are decent and that we all want a more peaceful world." Boyt's purpose is not to wallow in the memory of his sufferings, but to remind us that "with perseverance, life's worst hardships can be overcome." Whether those Americans who fought in World War II really represent their country's greatest generation is a matter for debate, but Boyt has neatly captured the essence of their experience with his simple maxim. It is possible to survive the darkest days without jettisoning one's morals or dignity. This is a legacy worth prizing.

GREGORY J. W. URWIN

[16] For an examination of the characteristics of American POW memoirs, see Robert C. Doyle, *Voice from Captivity: Interpreting the American POW Narratives* (Lawrence: University Press of Kansas, 1994).

PREFACE AND ACKNOWLEDGMENTS

Bataan: A Survivor's Story began as an idea in 1995. That year, I was teaching American history at a small junior college in Oklahoma City. As an "adopted son" of the Boyt clan, I had known Gene Boyt for many years. I was familiar with his role as a survivor of the Bataan Death March—although he had never recounted those events to me in detail.

That summer, while preparing a series of lectures on World War II, I invited Gene to visit my class and tell of his experiences. The offer sparked our initial discussions about his wartime service as well as other fascinating aspects of his life before and after the war. We soon realized that there was much more information than could be covered in a single lecture, but I was determined to preserve Gene's account for historians, scholars, and anyone else who wanted to know all that these men went through. So, in October 1997, I approached Gene with my notion of writing a book. He readily agreed, and, befitting his no-nonsense style, suggested we get right to work.

Gene and I live in different cities, so we communicated via audiotape. Gene recorded segments on a particular topic, and then sent them to me to edit and enter into a computer database. Each tape provided detailed and insightful information while whetting my appetite for elaboration, clarification, and historical context. So I drafted follow-up questions and mailed them to Gene. In turn, he responded with still more audio tapes. We continued in this manner for more than three years. In the end, we amassed some sixty hours of recordings covering every aspect of his remarkable life. The best of that wealth of material appears in the following pages.

• • •

This narrative record of the experiences of Gene Boyt during World War II is based solely on his recollections, perceptions, and opinions. Although every effort has been made to verify the historical accuracy of the information contained herein, a few of the dates, times, and locations represent close approximations. Likewise, the quotations attributed to certain people may be summaries of actual conversations or a composite of sentiments expressed by several individuals.

The term *Japs*, appearing in some quotations, reflects wartime usage. It refers to the Imperial Japanese military. Gene and I disapprove of the pejorative if it is directed at those contemporary Japanese not responsible for the conduct of the war.

• • •

Many people helped make this book possible. Betty Ruth Boyt, my long-time writing coach, mentor, and friend, taught me to employ the written word with clarity and passion. Kenny Tolman created the fine-looking maps of the Philippines and Japan. Charles Rankin, editor-in-chief of the University of Oklahoma Press, and his staff showed great patience and professionalism in guiding a pair of first-time authors through the complex and often daunting task of publishing a book. Jay Fultz deserves special thanks for copyediting the final draft. James Robinson provided some valuable legal advice. J. R. Trammell offered useful tips for reproducing and enhancing many of the photographs that appear in the book. Mary Anne and Robert Wolf read a rough draft of the manuscript and offered a host of invaluable suggestions for improving its sense and grammar. The following individuals offered invaluable help in locating, identifying, and obtaining the historical photographs included in the work: James Zobel, Hillary Levin, Melody Ann Lloyd, Rebecca Frisbee, Monica Abangan, and the still-picture reference team of the National Archives and Records Administration. As always, I am grateful for the incredible love and support of my mother, Elizabeth Gandy, and my wife, Amy. To all of you, I offer sincere and heartfelt thanks.

DAVID L. BURCH

INTRODUCTION

Bataan: A Survivor's Story chronicles my life, notable because of the harrowing events I witnessed as a soldier in the Pacific during World War II. But on a deeper level, this memoir recounts experiences that uniquely represent the "Greatest Generation" of Americans. Born in the wake of the Progressive movement of the early twentieth century, many of us were reared in crushing poverty during the Great Depression. As young adults, we served in a war unlike any other, one that changed the world profoundly and forever.

I devote much of the first chapter to what I learned while growing up amid hardship. The rest of the book deals mainly with my days as a prisoner of war. Following the surrender of American forces in the Philippines on April 9, 1942, the invading Japanese army captured me. After suffering through the infamous Bataan Death March, on which thousands of my comrades perished, I spent the remainder of the war in five POW camps that gave new meaning to the phrase "hell on earth." Now, more than sixty years later, I am among the last living survivors of Bataan, and I want to share my experiences.

I wrote *Bataan: A Survivor's Story* for two reasons. First, I hope to contribute to a more complete history of both the Bataan Death March and the broader POW experience. Second, I feel compelled to bring my story to later generations of Americans. I hope to demonstrate that, with perseverance, life's worst hardships can be overcome, and impossible odds can be beaten. So many World War II veterans are enduring proof of that, and if this book helps to commemorate their legacy, it will have been a rewarding undertaking.

During the twentieth century, the technology of war became more advanced and destructive than ever. I offer personal insight into the horror of combat. It is my hope that, short of compromising America's vital strategic interests, our leaders will seek to avoid war whenever possible.

Some may criticize my work as "Japan-bashing," the biased ranting of a bitter old man. But that is not my intention. I harbor no animosity toward the Japanese people and have tried to be as objective as possible. In an epilogue, I attempt to offer rational explanations for why the enemy treated us so brutally. Yet readers should not mistake this for a conciliatory tone. Quite the contrary; in recording their war crimes in complete detail, I hope to expose the Japanese guards for the monsters they were.

Bataan did not extinguish my faith in humanity. I still believe that most people, regardless of their race, are decent and desire peace. That is an idealistic goal, but we must strive for it anyway. A key to achieving global peace is to examine openly the barbaric deeds of the past, no matter how unpleasant, and vow not to repeat them. History is a window to the future, and I hope my story will help to expose many old wrongs. One day, if governments can truly learn from their mistakes, accounts like mine may no longer be told.

Finally, may this book serve as a cautionary tale. It is a stark illustration of the tragedy that occurs when people allow nationalistic zeal to override their basic humanity.

GENE BOYT

BATAAN

Let us run with perseverance the race marked out for us.

HEBREWS 12:1

CHAPTER 1

BEGINNINGS

Let me take it from the top. My name is Eugene P. Boyt (my friends call me Gene), and I was born on March 29, 1917, in Houston, Missouri. In those days, Houston was a tight-knit rural community of about two thousand people. It is located in the south-central part of the state, in the rolling hill country at the edge of Thorny Mountain.

My parents, who were natives of Missouri, had moved several years earlier to the oil fields of eastern Oklahoma, where my father worked as a tool-dresser on the old wooden cable-tool derricks. They returned to Houston prior to my birth that spring at the behest of my maternal grandfather, Dr. J. W. Phemister. He believed that good doctors were rare in Oklahoma, at least by his exacting standards, and insisted that my mother come home to deliver her second child in case complications arose. Grandpa Phemister was something of a legend in Houston. Working alone out of a two-room office on Main Street, he dedicated his life to providing medical care to the townspeople and was widely respected by them.

Fortunately, Grandpa was at the height of his skills when I arrived in the world. I am told my birth was "uneventful," although Mother might have described it differently. However, in the heat of the moment, the venerable Dr. Phemister made a minor mistake that has haunted me ever since: when filling out my birth certificate, he wrote down the wrong month for my birth. He listed me as having been born on *February* 29th instead of March 29th. Record-keeping procedures were not as thorough as they are today, and the error stuck. There was no Leap Year in 1917, so technically I was born on a day that did not exist! As a result, I later had trouble securing passports and other official documents. This gaffe was embarrassing for Grandpa, who prided himself on being a perfectionist. It was also the source of considerable good-natured teasing by my older relatives for many years afterward.

My parents were as different from each other as two people could be. The Phemisters were one of the most prominent families in Houston. J. W. and my grandmother, Julia, whom I also loved very much, had three daughters. My mother, Marguerite, was the oldest. Mom grew up in a large house, surrounded by most of the comforts available to a young lady of means. She was well educated, a graduate of Springfield Teachers' College in Springfield, Missouri. Mom had a life-long love of learning and following her graduation taught elementary school in the nearby town of Licking, Missouri.

Licking, with some one thousand inhabitants, was home to my father, Earnest Boyt. Dad's early life was much rougher than Mom's. His parents, Dan and Ollie, struggled to make a living on an eighty-acre farm while raising eight children.

The family was so poor that my dad had to quit school in the eighth grade to work as a laborer on a neighbor's farm. Determined to make a better life, he tried several jobs before finding his calling in one of the skilled trades of the oil field. If Mom was a true lady, Dad was all man, virile and self-confident. Although their match surprised many people, it is not hard to see how my parents settled upon one another. Each possessed distinctive qualities that complemented the other. Following a brief courtship, they married in early 1915.

The person who least understood my mother's attraction to my father was Grandpa Phemister. To put it kindly, he viewed Dad as an undeserving suitor and never understood why Mom forfeited the good life for the uncertain existence my father's job afforded her. But Mom genuinely loved him and was not troubled by his blue-collar status. She happily accepted her new life without looking back and set about providing a stable, nurturing home for her family. Ultimately, their marriage was blessed with three children. Wesley, the oldest, was born in December 1915. I came along next, and my sister, Betty Jane, joined us three years later, in 1920.

• • •

Shortly after my birth, Mom and Dad bundled me up, gathered their meager belongings into a beat-up Model-T Ford, and began the long trip back to Oklahoma. I was starting out like thousands of other boys born into similarly difficult circumstances. Frankly, there was little to suggest that my life held much promise, no hint of the incredible events fate had in store for me. I was just another poor kid who, like his father, might one day take an arduous job on some grimy oil derrick. That might have been my fate in an ordinary time, but I would reach adulthood in quite another time.

The early 1900s had been a time of dramatic change. Technological advancements, urbanization, and steep population growth transformed America. In the realm of politics, the nation's top Progressive thinkers—men like Theodore Roosevelt, Robert LaFollette, Hiram Johnson, and Woodrow Wilson—called for trust busting, home rules, referendum laws, consumer protections, and other reforms.

In August 1914, following the assassination of Archduke Francis Ferdinand, heir to the Austro-Hungarian throne, Europe erupted in the most horrific conflict the world had ever seen. Between 1914 and 1917, as World War I intensified, the United States struggled to remain neutral. But in April 1917, in the face of unrestricted attacks by German submarines on commercial shipping in international waters, America entered the war on the side of the Allies.

Once committed, the United States pursued its enemies with abandon. The production of armaments soared, and our troops headed "over there," vowing to achieve a victory so complete that it would end all wars. Unfortunately, reality was less noble. Eighteen months of brutal trench warfare followed, during which more than fifty thousand Americans were killed, before the U.S.-led Allies broke the stalemate and overwhelmed the reeling Central Powers.

After World War I, Americans celebrated joyously. The returning soldier was given a hero's welcome, and the country emerged as a global superpower. But the euphoria was short-lived. President Wilson could not win American entry into the idealistic League of Nations (an international body he envisioned as the benevolent guardian of the postwar world). With the collapse of the American-led peace effort, the European Allies dealt harshly with the defeated Central Powers. Their short-sighted strategy only created bitter nationalistic passions that would ignite an even more terrible conflict a generation later, one that would involve me and millions of other unsuspecting young men.

But in November 1918, that was still far away. I was just a toddler, and my parents were a typical young couple trying to make a living and raise a family. I doubt they even followed the events of World War I closely. They had more pressing concerns.

· · ·

My parents were right to be concerned about their future, for the end of World War I did not signal immediate prosperity for Oklahoma's petroleum-based economy. Things actually got worse. During the war, multitudes of derricks, pipelines, and refineries had sprouted up throughout the Sooner State. Experienced oil field workers like my dad were in demand. War was a boon for us; jobs were plentiful and wages were good. But when the fighting ended, so did much of the need for oil. Prices plummeted, and scores of drilling companies went bankrupt, casting many Oklahomans on hard times. The situation improved slowly throughout the "Roaring Twenties," but unpredictable economic cycles persisted. For years, it seemed the family just could not get ahead. Every time we were about to get out of debt, rig closings or layoffs occurred, and we were broke again.

My brother, sister, and I understood that times were tough but took them in stride. When Dad had work, he was an unselfish provider. When he was unemployed, we just did not have as much. That was the way of things growing up. Mom understood, too. Besides, it was not as if we were the only people who had to go without sometimes. Everyone else seemed to be in the same predicament. But as time passed, the constant uncertainty about the future began to strain my parents' marriage. Though I was only a boy, I wondered if the bond between them was strong enough to endure all the bad times.

Because of the unpredictable nature of Dad's work, we were constantly on the move. I'll bet we relocated a dozen times before I was ten years old. I cannot remember all the places my family called home. We lived in Braimen, Webb City, Ponca City, Maud, and St. Louis, all in Oklahoma; as well as a few other boomtowns that no longer exist. Because our home life was constantly in flux, I do not have fond memories of my early school days. I was always starting out in a new school, a terrifying prospect for a shy youngster like me.

Not surprisingly, I made few friends during those years, and that added to my sense of insecurity and isolation. What scant images I recall from elementary school are not pleasant: stern teachers, rote memorization, single-room schoolhouses that were poorly lit and always too hot in the spring, too cold in the fall.

Nevertheless, I enjoyed learning and quickly developed a love of reading—mostly history and adventure stories—that remains with me today. Since I did not make friends easily, books became my companions. They certainly offered a constructive means to pass many lonely hours. Growing up, I must have read hundreds of books. They sparked my imagination and broadened my horizons. Soon I dreamt of seeing the world, visiting exotic, faraway locales. Places unlike the despised Oklahoma boomtowns, which consisted of crowded rows of drab shanties built on the cheap.

But how was a poor boy going to see the world? I knew there had to be a way, and sometime during the mid-1920s, I started looking for it.

There was genuine love between me and my siblings, but I

was closer to Betty Jane because we were alike, having inherited Mom's gentle, thoughtful nature. Wesley was more like Dad: aggressive, self-assured, and somewhat domineering. I always felt inferior to him. Dad certainly related better to Wesley. I believed, no doubt irrationally, that Dad was not as proud of me because of my smaller stature and more introverted manner. The sibling rivalry never got out of hand, however. Wesley and I were different people. We accepted that. And in the end Dad did, too.

In the fall of 1929, when I entered the seventh grade, Dad found steady work in Asher, Oklahoma. We stayed there for the next two years, and I was able to complete junior high in the same school. That much-needed stability allowed my dormant social skills to blossom. I made some good friends and remember those days fondly.

My good times may have been just starting, but for America, the party was over. In October 1929, the stock market crashed, triggering the Great Depression. Fortunately, we oilfield brats were lucky in one sense: having lived all of our lives in uncertainy, we were more ready than most for the crisis. The country reeled from economic catastrophe, but it registered little more than a tremor in our neck of the woods. In fact, we were so poor I hardly noticed any downturn. We had my hard-working dad to thank for that. Because of his reputation as an accomplished tool-dresser, Dad was one of the few men able to keep working after the economy collapsed. So we stayed afloat—if just barely—through the early days of the depression.

All and all, my childhood was probably pretty normal. I was generally happy and well adjusted. Although bashful, I had a reputation for pleasantness and got along fine with other kids, if only because I did not say much. My parents were not stern disciplinarians, but then I never gave them much trouble. I was generally well behaved in school and remember getting licks only once, in the eighth grade, for "flirting" with some girls by throwing snowballs at them on the playground. For the most part, boyhood showed me a good time.

But I was growing up fast. In May 1931, as I stepped across the stage of the Asher Junior High auditorium to receive my eighth grade diploma, I felt the excitement of graduating from childhood.

. . .

That summer, when I was fourteen and preparing to enter high school, Dad lost his job on the oil well in Asher. He tried desperately to find other work, but the worsening depression made it impossible. Forced to sell most of our possessions, we went to Missouri to live on my paternal grandparents' farm.

Grandpa Boyt, who had once served as sheriff of Texas County, Missouri, had recently retired along with my grandma on a twenty-five-acre plot of land just outside Houston. Grandpa Boyt and my two uncles, John and Mack, who also lived there, tended the fields. Dad helped them, seeking drilling work wherever he could. He found little work, and we had very little money.

For the next year, the nine of us crowded into that farmhouse, pooling our meager resources to avoid starvation and praying for things to improve. I hated the arrangement. I was a restless teenager and, frankly, having to live with my grandparents was embarrassing. Do not get me wrong; I enjoyed spending time with them and do not know where else we could have turned in our time of need. But I longed for the days when we had our own home in Oklahoma.

I did not enjoy starting high school in Houston. We had

nothing—were often unsure of three meals a day—and I missed the familiar surroundings of Asher. Worst of all, I was the new kid again. I studied diligently (there was not much else to do) and was admired by my teachers, but I never clicked in that environment. Although I established a few friendships, none was close or enduring.

Our situation improved briefly in mid-1932, when Dad went back to Oklahoma to look for work. He found a job on a rig near Drumright, a small town in the east-central part of the state. When school ended in May, my brother Wesley and I hitchhiked back to join him. Dad was staying in a boarding house, and we moved in with him there.

Dad felt confident the job in Drumright would last awhile, so the three of us returned to Missouri in the Model-T to pick up Mom and Betty Jane. We then settled into the only house we could afford, an inexpensive piece of rental property located in the oldest part of Drumright. It seemed unlikely the family would stay there long, as transient as we were. But that was the last time we moved as a family, and I spent my remaining three years of high school in Drumright.

The continuing economic paralysis soon tightened its hold over the drilling business, and things got bad again. A few months after we returned to Oklahoma, Dad's well closed. After weeks of searching, he could not find another job. Being out of work was not unusual, but this time, faced again with unemployment, Dad did the unthinkable: he abandoned us. His cowardly act placed Mom in the terrible position of trying to provide for three children alone. Having been a house-wife most of her life, she had few marketable skills. Mom was qualified to teach school, but there were no teaching positions available. Grandpa Phemister sent us what money he could, but the depression had hit him hard, too, and he now had precious little to spare. In the fall of 1932, we hit rock bottom. It was only through the generosity of friends and neighbors that we managed to survive.

Mom must have been devastated by Dad's sudden departure. Yet, to her credit, she never berated him in front of us kids. Drawing on an inner strength that came from her deep faith in God, Mom carried on in the aftermath of unbearable heartbreak, and I admired her greatly for that.

Now on our own and unable to pay the rent, the four of us were evicted. We might have ended up on the streets if not for the generosity of a local banker, Coin Sellers (that really was his name), who allowed us to stay in a small house he owned. It was not much of a house—more like a dilapidated, two-bedroom shack. And we were still in need. Those were the only times during the depression that I remember regularly going to bed hungry. Sometimes, all Mom had to feed us was a little flour, lard, and water, which she used to make a flat, bland-tasting bread. Intense hunger was one of the worst feelings in the world, and I vowed to pull myself out of poverty and find a good steady job so I would not have to go hungry anymore. (After being captured by the Japanese in 1942, I endured systematic starvation, which was much worse than what I experienced during the depression.)

When the depression began in 1929, the federal government made no general provisions for aid to the needy. Not until President Franklin Roosevelt took office in March 1933 did aid become available to those who needed it, and my mother reluctantly joined Oklahoma's welfare rolls. Because she had three dependents, Mom received a cardboard box full of staple foods, such as milk, eggs, beans, flour, beets, hominy, and slab bacon, which was to last us thirty days. We were responsible for rationing it ourselves, and learned quickly to do so. Otherwise, we would still be hungry by the end of the month. My mother never received a handout of money, and she would not have expected one.

. . .

It is said that kids reared during the 1930s were "born adults" because of the many hardships they suffered at a tender age. That was certainly true in my case. Growing up is always tough; in the Great Depression it was extraordinarily difficult. I recall my three years at Drumright High School ("Depression High," as I call it) as rough ones. Our school was very short of money. We were taught only the basic subjects and frequently had to share textbooks and supplies with other students. Mom insisted that I study hard, however, and make good grades. She knew that education was a key to success and encouraged me to plan for the future. My attending college was never in question. It was always a given that I would go someday.

Although the depression limited the school's ability to offer extracurricular activities, Drumright High School had a football team, a band, and a Thespian Society. I was too small to play football, and while Drumright had a fine marching band that I would have loved to join, I could not afford an instrument. I did get to act in several plays, which was a lot of fun. Our productions were not elaborate. The props were rudimentary, consisting of hand-painted cardboard cutouts. For costumes, we borrowed clothes from our teachers. I was just an average actor, but the Thespian Society was a valuable experience for me. Performing in front of audiences helped me overcome my painful shyness, and I won the starring role in the senior play, a comedy called *All at Sea*. I was forever more self-confident and assertive as a result.

In the summer of 1934, before I started my senior year, my brother Wesley and I hitchhiked to Dad's new home in Shawnee, Oklahoma, to visit him and look for work. (Unlike today, hitchhiking was then a common and safe mode of transportation for the poor.) It was strange seeing my father again. When I had been with him last, he was a dominant force in my life, a trusted provider. Now, he was more like a stranger I was meeting for the first time—someone I was not sure I wanted to know.

Eventually, I forgave Dad for abandoning us. I still loved him, and in his own way he seemed sorry for what he had done, although he never apologized directly. The way he had hurt Mom was forever etched in my memory, however, and I felt very distant from him. Our interactions were awkward. He had lost my respect for him, and I did not miss him after that.

By that time, Dad had begun seeing a young woman named Thelma who was not much older than Wesley. We met her for the first time during our visit. She was pleasant and seemed to care for Dad, and I liked her well enough. But she could never hold a candle to my mother. There were no jobs in town for a couple of inexperienced teenagers, and to my relief, Wesley and I returned to Drumright after a few weeks.

Mom filed for divorce in 1936 (it took her that long to save the money to pay the court fees), and Dad and Thelma were married the following year. Thelma had a son from a previous marriage, but Dad ignored him. Dad's lack of parental involvement soon led to problems, and Thelma left him five years later. After his second divorce, Dad soon took a third wife, a nice woman named Emily. They had two children, Don and Patsy, who are both fine people. Dad stayed with Emily until his death in 1971. Mom, who never remarried, died in 1976.

Throughout high school, I could not wait to enter the larger world. Those years seemed to crawl by—until graduation approached. Then, suddenly, it seemed as though time had raced away, and I regretted not having enjoyed my last carefree days more.

High school had been special in many ways, and it marked the last time my siblings and I spent much time together. The summer after I graduated, Wesley left home and hoboed around the country on freight trains, doing odd jobs while trying to "find himself." After several years of drifting, he ended up in El Paso, Texas, and enlisted in the army shortly before the war. Military life suited him better than I expected. His assertiveness made him a natural leader, and he served honorably in Army Intelligence in Europe. Wesley ended up a career military man, retiring as a lieutenant colonel. With his wife, Bernice, he had two sons, Jim and Mike. He later worked as a newspaper editor and lived in Nevada until his death in 2000. Betty Jane also had a good life. She married her high school sweetheart, Robert Foster, who became an international businessman for Continental Oil Company. They spent most of their time in Singapore, Jakarta, and other exotic cities of the Far East. They had a son, Robert, and a daughter, Anne, who both became teachers. Betty Jane died of cancer in 1995.

Looking back, I am glad I did not realize what I was leaving behind in May 1935, when, as an energetic eighteen-year-old, I accepted my high school diploma. Had I foreseen the hard times ahead, I might have tempered my excitement about taking on the world. Facing life as an adult proved overwhelming at first, mainly because I had no idea what I was going to do next.

My wish was to go straight to college, but we were destitute, and I might as well have been planning an expedition to Mars. I knew that I would have to earn my own money for college, and to do that I needed a job, any job I could find.

A few days after graduation, I hit the streets in search of work. I interviewed with every possible employer, without luck. My situation was so desperate that twice a week I hitchhiked to the country club in Cushing, a small town about eight miles west of Drumright, in hopes of being hired as a golf caddie. Sometimes I was successful, but the competition for those assignments was considerable, and I often ended up walking the eight miles home with nothing to show for my efforts but a pair of blistered feet. If lucky, I got to carry a heavy golf bag for eighteen holes in the hot sun. For my services, I received a quarter—the going rate for caddies. It was a pitiful wage, but I was thankful to earn it. When times are that bad, you do what you must to survive.

Upon seeing my plight, an acquaintance suggested that I apply for the Civilian Conservation Corps (CCC). I had heard about the CCC ("the 3C's," as it was called) in high school, but had not thought to put in for it. Now the corps represented a new opportunity.

• • •

Launched in March 1933, the Civilian Conservation Corps was one of several relief programs created by the New Deal. It employed young single men between the ages of eighteen and twenty-two, assigning them to quasi-military units charged with improving the nation's public lands by planting trees; building small dams, bridges, and roads; fighting fires; and culling forests. The CCC ultimately employed more than two and one-half million youth, including me.

In late June 1935, two friends, Chester Morris and Gene

Smith, and I hitchhiked thirty miles to Sapulpa, the county seat of Creek County, Oklahoma, to enroll in the CCC. The application was a simple one-page document. I merely had to list my name, age, and the number of people in my family (which was now only three—my mother, sister, and me). The Social Security system was still on the drawing board, so none of us had Social Security numbers yet. There was no aptitude test or experience required. To qualify for the CCC, you simply had to be from a family on welfare. We did have to pass a cursory physical exam. A doctor simply took blood pressure and pulse readings and asked us a few basic questions about our medical histories. That seemed like a waste of time because most of those boys were so poor they had never been to a doctor and had no medical record.

Because our mothers were both on public assistance, Chester and I were accepted into the program. We simply signed the application and were in. Sadly, our friend Gene Smith was rejected because his parents were not on welfare. They were nearly as poor as the rest of us, but Gene's father was a mortician and his business was steady throughout the depression. Gene succeeded anyway, moving to Oklahoma City, where he had a productive career in the sheet metal industry.

About a week later, Chester and I received written notice to report to the Tulsa Railway Station. We kissed our mothers good-bye and hitchhiked to Tulsa.

Chester and I had no idea where we were going until we got to the depot. I suspected that our destination was far away because there were no CCC camps near Drumright. I learned later that the policy was to send boys to another state. The administrators knew that if we were far from home and became disenchanted, it would be a lot harder to quit the program. Our leaders were not hard-hearted; they arranged things for our own good. We all needed the income, which would be lost if we left the corps.

In Tulsa, Chester and I boarded a train that already held about two hundred enlistees from northern Texas. Looking around, I noticed that about a third of the boys were barefoot, and I pitied them. Most had never *owned* a pair of shoes. Peering down at the worn shoes on my own feet, I realized that I was not so bad off. I resolved to stop complaining about my "miserable" life and thanked God for many blessings.

We were bound for Fort Collins, Colorado, and a CCC camp near there. The trip took about a day and a half, and from Fort Collins we were trucked to a remote work site near Red Feather Lakes. There was no formal orientation at the camp. The leaders merely assembled us and explained that we would be working forty hours per week building a road up the mountainside. For our labor, we would receive thirty dollars a month, twenty-five dollars of which would be sent to our families back home, and five dollars of which we could keep. We were issued uniforms and assigned to barracks. The official dress uniform of the Civilian Conservation Corps was a khaki shirt, khaki pants, a black tie, and black work boots. We were provided several pairs of dungarees to wear while working.

Life in the Civilian Conservation Corps was highly structured. Each day began early—reveille at six o'clock—with us falling in outside the barracks. After counting off, we did twenty minutes of calisthenics. Then it was on to the bathhouse for a shower and shave before donning our work clothes and heading to the mess hall for breakfast. The workday began promptly at eight o'clock. Being on a forty-hour work schedule, we reassembled for lunch from twelve to one. Barring an emergency or unexpected problem, we stopped working at five o'clock each afternoon. On Saturday mornings, we assembled for inspection and were then dismissed for the rest of the weekend. The CCC had strict rules for personal conduct. No drinking or gambling was allowed in the compound, although both vices existed secretly, and young women were not permitted in the barracks. The danger of cigarettes was not considered back then, so smoking was tolerated everywhere.

My unit spent the summer of 1935 constructing roads near Red Feather Lakes—mostly with picks and shovels and a little help from bulldozers and graders. We also dynamited some sections of rock to clear the path en route. The tasks were easy to master, although there definitely is a right way and a wrong way to handle a pick and shovel, and doing it properly involves a certain skill. The work was physically demanding, but I was too happy to be earning money to complain. I do not feel that we CCC enlistees were exploited in any way. For the most part, the work we performed was well suited to the abilities of a bunch of kids with no experience.

My days in the CCC were good. I was young, carefree, and enjoying new friendships with fellows from other parts of the country. I was as healthy and muscular as I would ever be— even Dad would have been proud of me—and I fell in love with the rustic lifestyle of Colorado. Many years later, I returned to the area to build a cabin, which I still escape to periodically to recharge my spirit.

While working with the transportation engineers at Red Feather Lakes, I decided to make their profession my own. I greatly admired how they could look at a wooded hillside and picture a winding highway running up it, and then calculate the road's dimensions in exact detail, including the amount of time and resources needed to create it. Engineering appeared to be an ideal profession, one welding my fascination with technology to a practical career. It also seemed like important work, a way to leave a positive mark on the world. So I decided to become an engineer. My foremen later joked that they rued the day, because from then on, I peppered them with endless questions.

In the fall of 1935, my CCC unit was transferred from Fort Collins to a new camp near Fort Bowie, Arizona. There we built small brush dams to slow runoff from the desert rains. I liked Arizona immensely. The arid climate and picturesque terrain were much different from anything I had seen in Oklahoma or Missouri. It was pleasantly surreal to experience sunny, eighty-degree days in November and December. At Fort Bowie, we also had baseball and basketball teams, and I played on both. I managed to work my way up from laborer to assistant bulldozer operator, and when the lead bulldozer operator got sick, I was promoted to replace him. Instead of five dollars a month, I was now earning seven dollars and fifty cents a month in spending money, sudden wealth for me.

The following summer, I learned that a new camp was being started near Tucson and that a few of the boys from there would be allowed to attend the University of Arizona on a special scholarship in the fall. Thrilled about the possibility of attending a major college, I applied to the program immediately. Only two enlistees from each CCC camp in Arizona would be chosen, and the camp commanders made the selections. This was an opportunity I wanted very much, but I tried not to get my hopes up. There were so many other guys, I could not envision my being selected. To my surprise, I was one of the two chosen from Fort Bowie. I suppose my being a high school graduate, which most of the others were not, enhanced my chances, and our camp commander knew I was serious about getting a college degree.

Beginning in September 1936, I went into the city for four hours of class each weekday morning. I then returned to camp and resumed road building near what is now the popular Mt. Lemon resort area. I spent the following eighteen months that way.

Shortly after completing my third semester at the University of Arizona, I received a letter from Mom explaining that her sister, Serene McFarland, had invited me to come to Rolla, Missouri. She and my Uncle Arthur were willing to let me live with them, if I would do odd jobs around the house in exchange for my room and board. Unbeknownst to me, Mom had saved most of the twenty-five dollars a month I had been sending her. As a result, she had the two hundred and fifty dollars needed to pay my first year's tuition at the Missouri School of Mines (now the University of Missouri at Rolla), an engineering college located in Rolla. Thus, having earned three semesters of credit and the money to pay another year's tuition, I could enroll as a full-time engineering student in the fall.

I was ready to get back to my family, but quitting the CCC was not easy. During the depression, one did not give up a steady paycheck without apprehension. I was convinced that leaving was the right thing to do, however, and resigned from the CCC in August 1937. The camp commander hated to see me go but wished me luck and gave me a train ticket to Oklahoma. I stopped in Drumright for a quick visit with my mother and sister, and then hitchhiked about three hundred miles to Rolla.

Looking back, I must say that the Civilian Conservation Corps instilled pride in work that was worth every bit as much as the money paid. For me, the corps was a vital bridge to college. Incidentally, if you ever vacation in the Red Feather Lakes area, think of me. The road you will travel to get there is the same one my CCC unit built back in 1936, although it has been widened in the interim.

. . .

I went to Rolla in early September and settled into the McFarland house. My Missouri relatives were a bit aloof at first. But our relations soon improved, and I ultimately spent four pleasant years with them. Around Labor Day, I enrolled at the Missouri School of Mines (MSM). Established in 1871, MSM consisted of a dozen or so ivy-covered buildings in the oldest part of Rolla. The student body, which was overwhelmingly male, numbered about nine hundred. MSM was considered one of the best engineering schools in the country, so I was excited about completing my education there. The classes were small and the people friendly. Since engineering was the only major offered at MSM at that time, I had a lot in common with my classmates. That fall I met and developed a close friendship with a classmate named Bob Silhavy from St. Louis, Missouri. We majored in mechanical engineering and concentrated our electives in that area as well.

A prerequisite for attending MSM ultimately shaped my destiny. Because it was a federal land-grant college, all male freshmen and sophomore students were required to enroll in the army's Reserve Officers' Training Corps (ROTC). The ROTC program was created in 1920 in response to a shortage of front-line officers suffered prior to America's entry into World War I. By completing the course, which featured an optional advanced segment during the junior and senior years, a graduate was commissioned a second lieutenant in the Army Reserve and was then available for full-time active duty.

My first two years of ROTC training amounted to attending just another class, albeit a tough one. We received three hours of college credit but were required to attend five lecture hours per week, and we had numerous homework assignments and exams. It was a time-consuming class, but one of the best I ever took. As part of my training, I was issued an official uniform consisting of a green coat and trousers, white shirt, black tie, and green cap.

We did a lot of practice drills. Every Wednesday afternoon and on some Saturdays we held close-order drill, which is the basic marching routine taught to all beginning servicemen. It was part of our introduction to soldiering: how to fall in properly, how to dress our lines, how and when to salute and extend other forms of military courtesy, how to march in unison, and how to maneuver on command. These things were not difficult to learn, but it took diligent practice to perform them well. I worked hard and was good enough to be one of thirty cadets selected to march in an elite drill team at football games.

At the start of my junior year, I applied for admission to advanced ROTC. It was highly competitive with only thirty openings, and most of them were reserved for the best candidates. Nevertheless, by earning above-average grades and qualifying for the fancy drill team, I demonstrated my potential to be a good soldier and was accepted into the program. (Silhavy made it, too.) I never doubted that I wanted to complete advanced ROTC. By the end of my sophomore year, I had decided to pursue a career in the army.

The decision was made even easier because it represented the only way I could afford to finish my degree. Advanced ROTC paid seven dollars and fifty cents a month, pretty good money for a single guy in 1939. That money, supplemented by the fifteen dollars I earned for binding library books as part of a work-study program, meant I was earning the amazing sum of twenty-two dollars a month. I was in clover. While hardly rich, I could at least afford to buy some new clothes occasionally. My lack of a suit no longer mattered because, in advanced ROTC, I was awarded a fine dress uniform. That was a big perk, and it meant I could attend the annual military ball, the highlight of the spring season. I met a lovely young woman in Rolla who worked as a stenographer, and she accompanied me to the galas in my junior and senior years. Those were the only social functions I attended at MSM, and I enjoyed them immensely.

• • •

After my junior year, our ROTC unit was required to complete six weeks of training at Fort Riley, Kansas. It was intensive, full-time instruction with a military-engineering emphasis. We marched, negotiated the obstacle course, fired weapons, and practiced other field training. Being engineering troops, we learned how to build bridges and roads, and then used dynamite and TNT to blow them up. Instructors also showed us how to purify water (knowledge that proved critical to my survival at Bataan) and how to maintain sanitary facilities in the field.

An aspect of that summer course that I remember with painful clarity was the equestrian training. In 1940, the army was still using mounted regiments, and we drilled with the 8th Cavalry, which was stationed at Fort Riley. I was not a good rider. Although raised in Oklahoma, I had never been on a horse; neither had most of the other cadets. I was scared of horses, and they seemed to hate me. Luckily, the equestrian training lasted only about three hours a day for two weeks— just long enough for us to acquire a basic feel for the saddle.

On the first day of cavalry work, about forty of us entered

a large indoor riding arena. In the center stood forty fine-looking horses, and a weathered, stern-faced sergeant was mounted out front. He wasted no time showing us how to mount a horse the "army way." We were to stand on the horse's left side with the bridle in our right hand. On the count of one, we were to grab the saddle; on two, put our left foot in the stirrup; on three, swing ourselves over the horse's back; and on four, straighten up in the saddle, ready to ride. I tried to do it correctly. But I must have drawn the tallest horse ever to serve in the U.S. Army. I was only five feet six inches, so short that on the count of one, I could not raise my leg high enough to get my foot in the stirrup. On the count of two and three, everyone else was already in the saddle and I was still struggling to mount up. The crusty sergeant leapt off his horse, grabbed me by the seat of the pants, and "assisted" me into the saddle.

Then he got back on his horse and ran us through some basic maneuvers, gradually working his way up to a slow trot. Those horses were well trained; having been in service for years, they knew automatically to follow the sergeant's commands. After a few minutes, we moved up to a fast trot and things got dicey. As the horses picked up speed, the fellows began to bounce around in their saddles and holler. They did not realize that cavalry horses were trained to charge when their riders yelled, and as soon as they did, all the horses took off at a gallop! What ensued was a chaotic melee, with horses— some now minus their riders—darting to and fro and everyone exacerbating the situation by hollering "Whoa!" It was the low point of our training and probably the worst the U.S. Cavalry had looked since Custer charged at Little Bighorn. When the sergeant managed to straighten things out, he wasted no words.

A couple of days later the old sergeant led us outside on the trails that wound around the fort. We were riding in columns of two, with me and another guy bringing up the rear. When the sergeant called for the fast trot, my troubles began again. That giant horse of mine took off at a full sprint and ran right by the column! As we streaked past, the sergeant yelled for me to stop. I relayed the message via a frantic "Whoa!" But it did no good. The horse knew he was carrying a greenhorn and would not obey.

We galloped down the trail, eventually nearing a busy highway. Fortunately, the horse stopped. I sat in the saddle, relieved to be alive. But something must have startled the horse because he soon took off at a full charge back down the trail, now on a collision course with the other horses. So in mid-flight, here came the rest of the troop chasing me, and there I went right by them the other way!

After weaving through the oncoming traffic, my horse reached the stables, where he stopped as casually as if having returned from a soothing exercise walk. I, on the other hand, felt like I had just completed a steeplechase. I dismounted quickly before anything else went wrong. The sergeant, red-faced with anger, gave me some very intensive instruction in the art of riding a cavalry horse correctly. So ended my first week of training. But I refused to let that giant horse get the better of me. I worked hard the next week to improve my confidence and skill in the saddle. By the end of the fortnight, I had learned to ride respectably.

The equestrian training was a remarkable experience, especially since the program was ended a short time later. The tank would soon render the horse obsolete, and the futility of the modern cavalry was demonstrated with gruesome clarity two years later in the initial engagements of the Philippine campaign. There, the overwhelming advance of Japanese tanks and armored personnel carriers crushed those noble animals and their brave Filipino riders.

After the six weeks of training at Fort Riley, I hitchhiked to Oklahoma to pay a brief visit to my mother. Once back in Missouri, I got a job in the town of Lamar for the remainder of the summer. I was paid thirty-five cents an hour to conduct surveys for a contractor working with the Rural Electrification Authority.

. . .

Shortly before our graduation in the spring of 1941, my entire ROTC class was sent to Fort Leonard Wood, Missouri, for our final medical checkups. The physicals were comprehensive, but if you had normal blood pressure and were not flat-footed, you likely passed. I soon faced what I feared would be a serious problem.

Chronically skinny, I weighed only about 115 pounds. When someone told me that the minimum weight for an officer was 125 pounds, I panicked. How was I going to put on ten pounds in a couple of hours? Determined not to be denied a commission, I drank water continually and ate as many bananas as my stomach would hold while standing in line to weigh in. I had to run to the latrine numerous times, taking on more water after each trip, and the other men looked at me like I was insane. I do not think I gained an ounce and still would not have weighed 125 pounds with bricks in my pockets. But as it turned out, that did not matter. When I nervously stepped onto the scales, the officer in charge looked at the reading carefully, smiled at me, and then recorded my weight as 125 pounds. I am sure he did not misread the scales. The army needed as many second lieutenants as it could get, and probably I would have been passed had I weighed ninety pounds. Grateful for making the cut, I did not argue with him.

• • •

I completed my senior year of college in May 1941. At age twenty-three, I realized the biggest dream of my life, graduating from MSM with a bachelor's degree in mechanical engineering.

Immediately ordered into active duty, I was commissioned a second lieutenant in the army. I was an officer: small in stature but full of confidence, with an unwavering determination to serve my country honorably. I did not know how long my active tour of duty would last, but I was eager to be called up and felt no anxiety about it. Tensions were increasing overseas, and America's military needed to be on full alert. World War II had begun two summers earlier, on September 1, 1939, with Hitler's Nazi blitzkrieg on Poland, which added a global dimension to the war that Japan was waging in Asia. I remember hearing news of Germany's invasions of Scandinavia and France in 1940. We also watched films of the invasions in my ROTC classes. Although I was interested in the conflict's progress, it had not impacted me directly. My mind was fixed solely on finishing school.

As yet, there was not a lot of support in the United States for joining the Allied fight. Throughout 1941, America remained deeply divided about the war. Charles Lindbergh and his influential America First Society urged Yankee isolationism. On Capitol Hill, President Roosevelt nearly faced a congressional revolt when he reinstated the draft and began activating National Guard units. But I sensed that things would change soon. The threat to international security and the prospect of the U.S. entering the war increased with each Axis victory.

After graduation, our ROTC class spent several weeks at Fort Belvoir, Virginia, with the army's Sixth Instructor Class reviewing all of the training we had completed during the previous four years. At the end of the refresher course in early July 1941, our permanent assignments were posted. The morning the new stations were announced, Bob Silhavy and I scrambled to the bulletin board, elbowing our way through the excited crowd, to see where Uncle Sam was sending us. When we found our names, we were pleased. Both of us were going to the Philippines.

CHAPTER 2

SOLDIERING IN PARADISE

Although officially assigned to the Philippines, I probably could have requested an alternate assignment and avoided being imprisoned by the Japanese. But in the summer of 1941, I foresaw no negative consequences to overseas duty. I was intrigued by the thought of serving in an exotic locale and graciously accepted my new post. I knew little about the Philippine Islands, except that they were a U.S. territory gained during the Spanish-American War, but that unfamiliarity added an allure to the adventure. I looked forward to serving in the capital city of Manila.

My tour of duty had no definite timetable. Officers normally remained at one post for about three years and then moved on to diversify their training and experience. I therefore expected to stay in the Philippines about thirty-six months, then rotate back stateside, which suited me just fine.

I had a week before departing for the Orient, so the day my orders were posted at Fort Belvoir, I flew to Oklahoma for a pleasant two-day visit with Mom. For six years, while in the CCC and college, I had not seen her much, and we had a lot of catching up to do. Mom was proud of me and completely supported my going to the Philippines. If there was any fear in her mind, she never let it show. I thanked her for all she had done for me. Had I known how close I would come to never seeing her again, I would have expressed my love and appreciation more emphatically.

After leaving Oklahoma, I traveled by train with Bob Silhavy to St. Louis, Missouri, where Bob visited briefly with his parents. From there the two of us boarded a plane for San Francisco, the departure point for our journey to the Philippines.

During our flight to California, Bob and I met a very interesting older man who was seated next to us. His name was Mr. Trubereaux, and he was a mining engineer with properties located throughout Nevada and Utah. Mr. Trubereaux noticed the distinctive United States Corps of Engineers (USCE) insignia on our uniforms and proudly told us that he, too, had been a second lieutenant in the Army Corps of Engineers during World War I. Surprised to hear this, we listened captively as he entertained us with stories of his adventures in Europe a generation earlier. Mr. Trubereaux was inquisitive about our assignment in the Philippines, and we talked at length about what Bob and I would be doing there. As the plane landed, our gracious companion told us to come by his office in downtown San Francisco and he would help us see the city. We thanked him and promised we would. (While Mr. Trubereaux seemed like a very unassuming fellow, Bob and I found out later that he owned gold and silver mines throughout the West and was extremely wealthy. He was well known in the Bay area and apparently had a lot of clout there.)

Since 1899, San Francisco had been the primary port of dispatch for U.S. ships headed to the Orient. Upon our arrival in July 1941, Silhavy and I reported to the embarkation point at the Presidio. We were assigned quarters at the Hostess House and told that we would ship out four days later.

After settling in at the base, the two of us headed into town to visit Mr. Trubereaux at his elaborate office on Nob Hill. Delighted to see us, Mr. Trubereaux generously loaned us one of his personal cars to use while on leave. He even told us to bring the car back to his office garage each night and he would have it filled with gas, ready for us to take again the next day.

Mr. Trubereaux's hospitality helped me enjoy those days in San Francisco. Having been given permission to use the car all we wanted, Silhavy and I toured the place in style. We saw Alcatraz and Chinatown, rode on the famous trolley cars, and drove throughout the hilly metropolis, including several passes over the legendary Golden Gate Bridge.

As soon as we got to Manila, Bob and I sent Mr. Trubereaux a box of fine Filipino cigars as a token of our appreciation. After the war, we visited him on our way home. He was amazed to see us; he had followed the war carefully and could not believe that we had survived both the siege at Bataan and the Death March.

• • •

A few days later, Bob and I were among the twenty-five hundred servicemen who boarded the SS *President Cleveland* bound for the Philippines. The *President Cleveland* was a commercial cruise ship. Owned by the Dollar Line, it normally plied the

Pacific tourist trade but had been called into service to ferry military personnel overseas. Fortunately, we were the first group of troops to be transported on it. The crew, still accustomed to caring for civilian passengers, treated the officers like paying guests. The first-class accommodations were fine, and we officers ate in the sumptuous first-class dining room, which served some of the best food I have ever eaten. I sampled the whole menu before the voyage was over, including dishes I had never heard of, and was so pleased by the ship's bill of fare that I sent copies of it to my mom back home.

Somehow, another young officer and I were assigned to one of the few on-board staterooms. The spacious cabin was very clean and decorated in bright, inviting colors. We had comfortable twin beds, a portal, and a private bath. My roomy and I knew immediately that someone had made a mistake, for our lodgings were stellar compared to those of other officers. The old army adage "RHIP"—Rank Has Its Privileges—was in effect, and had any majors or colonels found out where we were staying, we would have lost that fine setup immediately.

Needless to say, my roommate and I kept quiet. That was easy for him, because he had no friends on-board. But my buddy Bob Silhavy was bunking with about forty other junior officers in a makeshift barracks with cramped beds and a communal bathroom. His area of the ship was so crowded that he could only take a shower once every couple of days. Wracked with guilt, I told Silhavy about my room and, after swearing him to secrecy, let him use the tub whenever he wanted.

Throughout the voyage I feared losing that prime cabin. But luckily, no one discovered the arrangement. As we sailed on toward the Philippines, I became convinced that my fortunes were on the rise.

The voyage to the Philippines took nearly three weeks, during which I was simply a passenger with no official duties. It was a pleasant vacation. I slept late, read a few books, sunned myself on deck, played poker with friends, watched the movies that were shown nightly in the main stateroom, and just relaxed before starting my new job. The seas were calm, and I had a splendid time.

The first phase of the trip, from San Francisco to the United States naval base at Pearl Harbor, Hawaii, took about seven days. Pearl Harbor was a large installation, but it did not make a profound impression on me. In those days, it was simply another naval base. That was five months before the surprise Japanese attack on December 7, 1941. It turned out that I was among the last groups of Americans to see Pearl Harbor as it was before the war: pristine and inviolate, a proud symbol of America's maritime strength, not the harbor of smoking debris and death it soon became.

We soon left Hawaii for Guam, a five-day voyage. When we left Hawaii, the major in charge ordered that no alcohol be allowed on ship. Since many of the young officers liked to drink, they had already smuggled stashes of liquor aboard. But most had run out by the time we reached Guam, our next port of call. So when the ship docked, they went ashore to restock their supplies of booze. To get the stuff back on the ship, men slipped it into their clothes or duffle bags. Some even tried to hide it by wearing their long dress overcoats, attire that looked quite suspicious in the tropics.

My buddy, Bob Silhavy, drew "officer of the deck" duty. That meant he had the unenviable job of ensuring that no contraband, including alcohol, was brought aboard the *President Cleveland*. When the others returned from shore, Silhavy asked them if they were carrying any spirits. They lied and said, "No." Silhavy knew they were fibbing but did not deny them passage. If he had, those men would have gotten back at him somehow before we reached the Philippines.

I did not leave the ship in Guam because we stayed there only four hours. That was just long enough to drop off mail and take on freight before setting sail again.

I remember being up on deck on our last afternoon at sea. I walked around serenely, anticipating our arrival in Manila the next day. Below the water's surface, twin propellers thrust the ship forward with swift, reassuring gyrations. A refreshing breeze swirled overhead, filling the ventilation sails. Looking back across the *President Cleveland* from the bow, I saw the Stars and Stripes waving proudly in the sunlight. Just ahead lay the start of what I thought would be a long, successful service career. I could not hide my enthusiasm, for I was just hours away from an island paradise full of promise.

•   •   •

When we made port at Manila, I caught my first glimpse of the Orient. The Filipino capital was a hectic metropolis of some ten million people; virtually every race and nationality was represented there. Manila Bay was strategically located, a hub of international commerce. The docks were filled with freighters that ran the region in search of trade. The city's streets teemed with traffic: motorcycles; jitneys, which were small, motorized vehicles converted into mini-buses; taxis; small horse-drawn carriages called *callases*; bicycles; and pedestrians.

In many ways, Manila was a magnificent and traditional Polynesian city. Yet it showed signs of rapid growth and transition. Some areas were extremely impoverished, packed with overcrowded shanties; others were deluxe and ultramodern, complete with Western-style high-rise buildings. The highly stratified Philippine society consisted of only two classes—the wealthy and the poor. To me, Manila presented an alien atmosphere, but I found it fascinating and soon came to appreciate the wonders of its diverse culture.

I reported first to Fort Santiago, pending my permanent assignment. Built by Spanish conquistadors more than three centuries earlier, Fort Santiago was an ancient Spanish bastion in the oldest part of the city. The large, thick-walled edifice, complete with picturesque gun turrets overlooking the bay, housed the administrative offices of the U.S. Army's Far East Command.

As often happens to young soldiers posted overseas, my friend Bob Silhavy and I were split up. Bob was ordered to a base in southern Luzon, about two hundred miles from Manila. I assumed we would see each other often in the coming weeks. In fact, we were not reunited until after the war began four and a half months later.

Fort Santiago was also headquarters for General Douglas MacArthur, the supreme commander of American forces in the Far East. I was not a fan of General MacArthur. I remember vividly the disappointment I felt in 1932 over the infamous Bonus Army incident. At the height of the depression, MacArthur, then the army chief of staff, led troops in a bloody raid to remove forcibly a large group of World War I veterans who had marched on Washington to lobby Congress for financial assistance. MacArthur's actions, while directed by President Herbert Hoover, angered millions of Americans and haunted the general for the rest of his career. Yet, at the same time, I was impressed by his imposing persona. His entourage included numerous high-ranking officers, military police, and other notables who accompanied him wherever he went. I did not know much about General MacArthur at that point and remained ambivalent toward him. I just assumed that he knew what he was doing and felt confident in his command. I was mistaken.

Although I never met General MacArthur, I did see him in person several times as he traveled throughout Manila. His regal band always stopped traffic. One day, not realizing that MacArthur was passing behind me, I failed to salute and was severely reprimanded by a senior officer. From that moment on, until I left Fort Santiago, I watched out for MacArthur.

About ten days after arriving at the fort, I was ordered to report to Clark Field, located about sixty miles north of Manila, where I would be project engineer. I was ecstatic. Project engineer at Clark Field was an ideal assignment for an ambitious young engineer like me. It seemed I had really lucked out this time.

• • •

Clark Field was a bomber installation and the largest air base in the Philippines. Located two miles from Fort Stotsenburg, Clark Field was home to more than three thousand servicemen, most of them Army Air Corps personnel. The commander was Colonel Lester J. Maitland, a renowned American aviator. In 1927, Maitland and Albert E. Hegenberger became the first men to fly nonstop from San Francisco to Hawaii. Fifteen years later, Maitland still cut an impressive figure. He was tall and carried a swagger stick, which accentuated his powerful presence, but he did not strike me as being pompous like MacArthur.

My immediate supervisor at Clark Field was Colonel Wendell Fertig. Colonel Fertig, a former civilian mining superintendent, was also an admirable man. When called into active service from the army reserve in 1941, Colonel Fertig proved a highly competent leader. He was eventually ordered to Corregidor. Shortly before its surrender in May 1942, he escaped to the island of Mindanao and earned fame by commanding guerrilla forces against the Japanese.

Colonel Fertig explained that, since he was being transferred to Manila, I would be responsible for overseeing all construction projects at the base. I was honored. The assignment was challenging, and I promised him I would give it my all.

I was also assigned a permanent residence at Clark Field. Like my new job, the house was unexpected. My quarters were located adjacent to the runway on Officers' Row, a line of comfortable bungalows with private rooms and a staff of Filipino servants. Senior officers and their families had occupied the house until the spring of 1941, when General MacArthur, out of safety concerns, ordered all dependents stateside. Colonel Fertig and a second lieutenant had been living in the bungalow, and when I arrived, I took Fertig's place. Surrounded by tall palm trees and a colorful flower garden, the bungalow had four bedrooms, a bathroom, a kitchen, and a screened-in porch along the front and on one side. I was comfortable there and was not subject to snap inspections or the like. I simply went to my construction site in the morning and, after completing my work, came home and was on my own until the following day.

• • •

American troops continued arriving en masse in the Philippines during the late summer of 1941. In September, the support staff for the 19th Bomber Group arrived and brought with it two officers who moved into our bungalow—a lieutenant colonel named Laughinghouse and a major who was a physician. As is typical in the Philippines, the place was soon invaded by legions of gecko lizards. The gecko's name was taken from the unique croaking sound it made. The crafty little reptiles constantly climbed up the walls, hid in shoes, or hung from the ceiling. I was mildly afraid of them at first, and the others laughed at my uneasiness. But the geckos were harmless, and, since they ate a lot of mosquitos, they were welcome.

Our bungalow employed six full-time servants: two house-boys, two *lavendaros* (washwomen), a cook, and a gardener. All were loyal attendants who fawned over us to the point that I felt like royalty. The old cook, who was Chinese, supervised the servant crew. He was regarded as one of the best chefs on base. I was skeptical of this claim at first because he did not fit my image of a gourmet. He chewed betelnut constantly and had no front teeth. The cook did not speak English and was quite gruff, making it plainly known that he wanted no one "trespassing" in his kitchen. But once I tried his meals, I was a believer; the food was excellent. His specialty dessert was baked Alaska, which he made frequently. It tasted mar-velous, and I always had seconds.

That is, until one day when I happened by the kitchen while the aged chef was preparing a baked Alaska for the evening meal. He had the delectable torte up on the coun-tertop and was using a knife to form a beautiful decorative pattern with the meringue. I licked my lips in anticipation. But then he took a mouth-full of water and, through that hole in his front teeth, squirted it onto the cake to form a glisten-ing for the final touches on the frosting. Suddenly not very hungry, I tried to forget how many times I had eaten one of his baked Alaskas. I loved that dessert but always politely passed on it after that.

The Philippines were wildly exotic. The most fascinating

element of my stay was an encounter with a tribe called the Negritos. The Negritos, who were Filipino aborigines, were Pygmies. As adults, they stood only about four feet tall and had dark skin and kinky black hair. By Western standards, their lifestyle was very primitive; they dressed in loincloths and hunted with bows, arrows, and spears. When I arrived at Clark Field, a small band of Negritos was living at the edge of the jungle just west of Fort Stotsenburg. The Negritos were quite a novelty, and most newcomers ventured out to see them. I, too, visited them in September 1941.

Upon first seeing the Negritos, I was amazed. They looked like creatures from a fairy-tale. Since the Negritos spoke no English, we communicated by pantomime. I wanted to buy some of their weapons as souvenirs, but the Negritos lived so simply that money meant nothing to them. However, I brought along a small mirror and some matches, items the Negritos valued highly. After a bit of haggling, I agreed to swap the matches for an exquisitely crafted bow and arrow set, which, unfortunately, I later lost to the Japanese.

• • •

As project engineer at Clark Field, I oversaw the work of local contractors who were reimbursed through the Army Finance Office (AFO), located at Ft. Stotsenburg. The AFO made monthly payments based on my estimates of the work completed. The Filipino firms hired their own employees and determined their salaries. My work hours were fluid and unpredictable. I set my own schedule but cut myself no slack, working an average of fifty hours a week. The overtime was necessary to keep up with the intense demand for construction. But the work was extremely interesting, and I was driven to succeed.

In October 1941, we were to receive a squadron of B-17s, the sleek four-engine bombers that became the high-altitude workhorses of the air war, and our first priority was to build a new runway to accommodate them. Clark Field had only one landing pad, made of graded dirt. The new runway was to mirror the existing one, which we were extending to about five thousand feet in length. Dirt runways seem incredibly simple today, but the planes of that era were not nearly as fast or delicate as modern ones, which could not land on such a surface. They would crash and be lost. While work on the new runway occupied most of my time, the contractors were also building dozens of earthen structures called revetments, which resembled individual airplane hangars. Built in two sizes, large ones for the B-17s and smaller ones for the fighters, the revetments were U-shaped and wide enough to hide a single plane in the event of an enemy air attack. They were moderately effective against bomb shrapnel (although useless in the event of a direct hit), and they provided good protection against strafing machine-gun fire.

Neither the runways nor the revetments were difficult to construct with the use of bulldozers, graders, and other standard equipment. The work required leveling and grading long stretches of land, but it was a relatively easy undertaking, no more complex than the CCC road-building projects I had worked on, and I felt well in control of things. Minor problems arose, but I handled each in turn, gaining confidence and enjoying myself immensely.

· · ·

Summers in the Philippines are very hot and humid. Daytime temperatures often reach 100 degrees Fahrenheit. In the 1940s, there was no air-conditioning, but overhead fans were standard in all of the buildings on base. When I went home for lunch each afternoon and for dinner in the evenings, I took off my sweaty uniform and had one of the houseboys give it to a lavandaro, who then handwashed it. The houseboy had another uniform cleaned, pressed, and starched, waiting for me to put on. I changed clothes two or three times a day and tried always to look sharp.

Those two houseboys also kept our bungalow looking sharp. Every morning they moved the furniture, then tied coconut husks to the bottoms of their feet and skated across the hardwood floor to polish it. This unique method of waxing worked well, and the floors always glistened like mirrors.

I also had a private jeep and my own Filipino chauffeur. The chauffeur was to protect the army from liability in the event of an accident. Only a fool drove himself around Manila. The roads were jam-packed with traffic, and if you had a wreck you could find yourself in big trouble with local officials. Also, I needed someone with me who spoke the native languages and who could guide me via the shortcuts from place to place.

Incidentally, only one road into Manila was paved. During rice-harvesting season the Filipino women placed their rice on large bamboo mats in the road so that the traffic would crack its husks. Then they could winnow the rice in the wind, and it was ready to prepare.

About a month after I arrived at Clark Field, Major Harry Fischer, who later served as area engineer for northern Luzon Island, became my supervisor. Major Fischer spent most of his time in Manila attending to the details of design and planning. He did not interfere with my work, and I was pleased when he quickly got me promoted to first lieutenant. I was awarded the promotion partly because of my experience and satisfactory work. But I think Major Fischer wanted to give me more authority because I had no higher-ranking officers working with me.

. . .

I never got homesick while in the Philippines. The fact that I had gone away at a young age to work in the CCC helped me accept separation from my family. I still loved them tremendously but was busy pursuing the career I had spent years training for. Luckily, the mail service from the Philippines was good (correspondence usually reached me within two weeks), and I wrote home often and received many letters from my relatives. Mom was an especially loyal pen pal. She even sent me articles from the local newspaper so I could keep up with all the smalltown gossip. Mother's situation had improved since the depression. She was now a successful businesswoman, managing the only bus station in Drumright, Oklahoma.

Since I had a lot of disposable income and did not need to send money home, I lavished my loved ones and myself with gifts. Products were inexpensive in Manila, and I took advantage of the cheap labor market. I purchased beautiful tailored sharkskin suits for only twenty pesos (roughly ten American dollars). I ordered high-quality tailored uniforms so I did not have to wear the baggy ones available at the PX.

I also remember buying a large roll of pongee silk, which would have cost a fortune in the States, for only twenty dollars and sending it to my grandmother in Missouri. The military allowed us, when mailing things home, to write "Soldier's Gift" on the parcel and thus avoid paying customs duties. It took about six weeks for a package sent from the Philippines to reach America.

Near Clark Field was a humble village called Angeles. Its

fifteen thousand Filipino peasants mostly worked at various jobs in and around the post. Vice was prevalent in Angeles, and the place became infamous for its thriving red-light district. In fact, due to the high rate of venereal disease among U.S. troops in the summer of 1941, the town was declared off-limits to American personnel. MPs were posted around the bars and brothels to ensure that the ban was enforced. Once, when I attended a banquet in Angeles with several other officers from Clark Field, I was shocked to discover how far our Filipino hosts would go to fulfill the men's most lascivious fantasies.

A high-ranking Angeles official, who was also one of my contractors, was our host that night, and after dinner, he announced that the city had a grand new building project underway. As an engineer, I listened closely. The official knew that many young officers were stationed at Clark Field and scores more would be coming in the weeks ahead, so he and other local residents wanted to show their gratitude by building a "recreational bar and inn" for them. It would be a luxury hotel open only to American officers. In a proud tone, he assured us that beautiful girls (prostitutes), whom a doctor would certify as disease-free, would be available there at all times.

We were astonished. But there was more. City officials had decided to call the new establishment "Kingsville," after General Edward P. King, commander of Fort Stotsenburg. The leaders of Angeles thought they were honoring him. A diplomatic disaster was averted only when the senior officers explained why the naming would not be appropriate.

A few days later, I answered a knock at the door of our bungalow to find a well-dressed Filipino chauffeur standing there. He handed me a note from a high-ranking Angeles official that included a fancy gift card, printed in English, identifying me by name and stating that, when presenting it at the new "recreation hall," I was never to be charged for services.

Naturally, I showed the card to my roommates and joked that until now they had never known a man who had a free lifetime pass to a whorehouse! I would love to have kept that gift card as a souvenir, but the Japanese soldier who took my pocketbook following our surrender confiscated it.

Standards of virtue were not all that distinguished our two lands. The Philippines had a much lower standard of living than the United States. All but the privileged few existed in simple thatched huts. Yet most Filipinos seemed content, and they understood that we Americans were good for their economic and military interests.

However, a small but formidable block of Filipinos genuinely resented Americans. Prominent among them were the Hukbalahaps, or "Huks," who were Communist revolutionaries. Though not numerous, they engaged in guerrilla warfare with the pro-Western Filipino Constabulary, an .elite police force similar to the Royal Canadian Mounted Police. Like modern terrorists, the Huks were a constant yet invisible threat, clawing at the fringes of society. Fortunately, they were not representative of the majority of Filipinos, whom I trusted and among whom I felt comfortable.

"Comfort" may be the best word to describe my first months in the Philippines, and I remember the late summer of 1941 as a tranquil season. In the evenings I often sat outside with a cool drink in hand, leisurely admiring a glowing sunset over the mountains to the west of Clark Field. On weekends I took lazy naps under the relaxing solace of a ceiling fan, bamboo matting draped across the windows to provide extra relief from the heat. As summer ended, pleasant days continued to pass in an unbroken pattern. The weather was always balmy, the work exciting, and the breeze renewing. Indeed, with the exception of the early 1950s, when I was raising a young family back home, my prewar days at Clark Field represented the best time of my life. I was content to have things stay just as they were, forever.

• • •

All about me, however, the largest military buildup in the history of the Philippines was underway. Troops continued to arrive throughout the fall, and in October the 194th Tank Battalion and the 200th National Guard, an antiaircraft regiment from New Mexico, set up positions around Clark Field and at Fort Stotsenburg. Air Corps personnel were coming by the hundreds, including more administrative and support staff from the 19th Bomb Group, which included the squadron of B-17s we were to receive that month. The 803d Engineering Battalion, whose duty was airfield construction, also arrived. The engineers formed a good, well-supplied unit. Their headquarters was located at Clark Field, and three of their companies were sent to various spots in the Philippines to build additional airfields. Members of the 803d were a big help to me. Although they were not involved directly in my assignments, I went to them with numerous questions related to my work. I was new, and having their expertise available was a big relief. I also enjoyed talking with other engineers who understood and appreciated my mission at the base.

I stayed busy during the fall, with multiple construction assignments underway. In addition to the runways and revetments, we built roads, bridges, and other infrastructure throughout Clark Field. We even contracted for the fabrication of plywood replicas of our aircraft. These "dummy" planes were virtually indistinguishable from the air, and they could be placed strategically along the runways to divert bombs from the actual planes. (This tactic was so effective that the Japanese wised up and adopted it, with slightly less success, later in the war.)

My schedule became even more demanding when I received preliminary orders to build barracks for *thirty thousand* incoming Air Corps troops. This was bad news for my roommate, the lieutenant colonel, who was an avid golfer, because it meant I would have to clear the golf course at Fort Stotsenburg to make room for the new lodgings.

• • •

That fall I was privileged to meet one of the islands' most famous residents, Captain Hornbostel, an American known throughout the Philippines. To me he seemed very old, but he was probably not more than seventy at the time. Captain Hornbostel had come to the Philippines during the Spanish-American War and remained. Upon leaving the army, he joined the Filipino Constabulary and rose quickly through its ranks, eventually becoming commandant. Now retired, he occasionally entertained Wendell Fertig and me in Manila.

Hornbostel was remarkable on many levels. Because his knowledge of the Philippines was so extensive, he served as a civilian advisor to the U.S. Army. When discussing military topics, he could anticipate every question and be ready with an insightful reply. He also possessed a disarming sense of humor.

One evening in late October, Wendell Fertig and I were with Captain Hornbostel as he briefed an engineering lieutenant on a special assignment laced with intrigue. The lieutenant was leaving the next morning for Zamboanga, the southernmost major city on the island of Mindanao. His plan was to make his way alone through the dense jungle to a remote point on the coast. There, he was to recruit Filipino laborers and construct a runway that B-17s could use as a stopover point between Clark Field and Australia.

Captain Hornbostel knew the mission would be dangerous because a ferocious Muslim tribe known as the Moros inhabited the region. The lieutenant wanted to take his rifle and .45-caliber pistol for protection, but Captain Hornbostel, who knew Moro customs well, cautioned emphatically against it.

"No," he said. "You must not do that. The Moros will kill you for the weapons. As strange as it sounds, you're safer if you go unarmed."

Hornbostel told the young officer to keep only enough money on him to pay the workers each day. If he did that, went unarmed, kept away from the Moro women, and treated his men with respect, he would be safe, Hornbostel assured him.

When we surrendered the Philippines to the Japanese a few months later, the scheme to forge an undisclosed runway on Mindanao was abandoned. I do not know what happened to that lieutenant, but if he followed Hornbostel's advice, he may have eluded capture and remained in the southern jungle throughout the war. For his part, when the siege at Bataan began the legendary Hornbostel was assigned to my battalion headquarters. Despite his advanced years, he made the Death March and survived years of captivity in Japan. He held up better than most men half his age.

• • •

During the last week of October, the long-anticipated squadron of B-17s finally arrived at Clark Field. The planes came from San Francisco by way of Hawaii, Wake Island, Midway, and Australia. We had hurried to finish the runways in time and both strips were operational when they arrived. It was a major event, and I went out to watch some of the B-17s come in. They were the largest and most powerful bombers the U.S. had ever produced. Their raw, majestic force was awe-inspiring. The planes were so low on fuel, however, that they landed in two directions, almost on top of each other, on both runways. They all made it safely, a significant accomplishment at the time. Having the B-17s at Clark Field, using *my* runways, was personally satisfying. I felt proud—and secure.

But one night about a week later, I was unnerved when one of the new B-17s went down during test maneuvers. The plane was making passes over the runways to allow the 200th to properly set the searchlights for their antiaircraft guns. When the pilot flew into the path of the powerful beams, he became disoriented, went into a vertical dive, and crashed. I was watching a movie in the theater at Clark Field when it happened. When we heard the shattering explosion, everyone raced out to see the flaming metal and thick black smoke. Fire crews rushed to the scene, but there was little they could do. The plane was destroyed and the crew killed instantly. The impact also left a large crater in the runway that my men had to scramble to fill at daybreak.

The next night, with the runway once again in use, Colonel Maitland and the squadron commander went up in another B-17. They had the 200th repeat the scenario in order to see what had happened. The two leaders made numerous passes into the powerful lights but had no problems. The exact cause of the crash was never determined. Nevertheless, I always admired Colonel Maitland's courage in troubleshooting to prevent another disaster.

• • •

The B-17's fatal crash was a grim reminder that, even in an island paradise, death shadows those in the military. An incident a few days later, on about November 20th, brought that fact even more clearly into focus. I had arrived home at noon that day. As we were eating lunch, one of my roommates said that all officers were to assemble on the main runway at 1 P.M. for a special announcement from Colonel Maitland.

We went there at the appointed time and joined about two hundred others in the center of the runway. MPs were stationed all around, indicating to me that something big was happening. After a few minutes, Colonel Maitland climbed onto a table so he could see the entire group.

In a calm, measured voice, he said, "From this moment on, Clark Field is on a war footing." No one was allowed to leave the base, and if we traveled to Fort Stotsenburg, we had to inform headquarters in advance.

"Every plane will be armed," Colonel Maitland continued. "Every bomber will carry a full load of bombs and armaments." When crews patrolled the China Sea, they were to attack any ship failing to respond properly. "Likewise, if an unknown plane does not respond correctly, engage it and shoot it down."

Colonel Maitland's words sent shock waves through the assembly. I looked at my roommate in bewilderment. My engineering duties kept me somewhat out of the loop, so the others had to fill me in. Apparently, Japanese observation planes had been spotted flying over the Philippines for the past several weeks, but the aircraft flew too high and fast for our fighters to reach them.

Colonel Maitland obviously felt that the Japanese were about to make a move. Thus, Clark Field was alerted to danger *two weeks* before the attack on Pearl Harbor. If Colonel

Maitland had advance warning, it is certain that General MacArthur did as well. And still we suffered a disaster at Clark Field. To this day, I do not understand how it happened.

I was surprised but not shocked by the announcement, and I do not recall being particularly frightened. Although we were now on a war footing, I did not think about war actually happening. I loved life in the Philippines so much that I had become oblivious to Japanese intentions. I should have known better because, by late 1941, the war had already engulfed Europe, North Africa, and Asia. As a precaution, I gave my rifle and pistol an extra cleaning. That made me feel I had done all I could to prepare for what lay ahead, though I always kept the weapons in good shape. Otherwise, I just went on with my work. A few Filipinos got scared, quit their jobs, and returned to the countryside. But most of them stayed with me. I doubt they knew what danger they were in at Clark Field. My laborers just wanted to support their families and survive. Unfortunately, not all of them did.

• • •

I caught a bad cold in the first week of December. For several nights starting around December 3, I was up with a loud, hacking cough. The doctor who lived in our bungalow finally told me to go to the hospital at Fort Stotsenburg, where he arranged for treatment of my respiratory infection. He likely did this on orders from the lieutenant colonel, who was tired of being kept awake by my incessant coughing.

Being sent to the infirmary upset me because I had so much construction underway, but I could not disobey a superior officer. Reluctantly, I reported to the medical unit at Fort Stotsenburg on the morning of Saturday, December 6, 1941. I tried to explain to the nurses that I did not need to be in the hospital. Unyielding, they promptly ordered me to bed. I refused to stop working, because I has no second-in-command to supervise operations. My foremen came to the hospital to get instructions for the day's assignments.

Looking back, I should not have worried so much about the construction projects. The fact that I was pushing myself so hard undoubtedly contributed to my illness. After a good day's rest on December 6, I realized the break was good for me. The holidays were approaching, and I needed to slow down. There was no crisis at Clark Field; everything was under control, and I had no reason to feel so stressed. After a little more relaxation, I would be fitter than ever.

So, on the night of Sunday, December 7, (still December 6 in Hawaii, on the eastern side of the International Date Line), I settled into a peaceful sleep, secure in the belief that I would soon be back to my routine, possibly even by morning.

CHAPTER 3

TO BATAAN

"Lieutenant Boyt, wake up!" Ashen moonlight flowed through the window behind my bed, indicating that it was not yet dawn on Monday morning. As I opened my eyes slowly, I felt the touch of soft hands on my forearm. "Lieutenant, you have to get up!"

A young American nurse was leaning over me. "What is it?" I asked.

"Pearl Harbor's been attacked!"

"When?" I struggled to bring my thoughts into focus.

"A short time ago."

"Was it the Japs?"

"Yes. Does this mean war?"

"I'm afraid it does."

Around 8 A.M., the head nurse called out the names of all ambulatory patients, including me. Those who could walk were declared "cured" on the spot—what I had wanted all along. Since we were fit for duty, about half of us got dressed and reported to our stations at once.

• • •

Making my way back to Clark Field, I saw that the distressing news from Pearl Harbor had spread like fire. There was a great sense of urgency, as soldiers and vehicles moved quickly in all directions. It seemed plans were underway to shore up other posts throughout the islands, and the troops at Fort Stotsenburg were in full battle dress, preparing to deploy.

As I reached my office, I wondered tensely if these preparations were merely a precaution or the prelude to a full-scale invasion. I relaxed a bit once I got inside and started hearing from my contractors what had happened in my absence. Most of our conversation was about the attack on Pearl Harbor. Like me, the men did not know what to make of it. I tuned the radio to a Manila station that was providing continuous coverage of the situation in Hawaii. According to news reports, at just before 8 A.M., Honolulu time, Japanese carrier planes attacked the U.S. naval base at Pearl Harbor, sinking four battleships and killing some 2,500 servicemen. Among the vessels lost were the *Arizona* and *Oklahoma,* news that shook me. I had lived, worked, and been educated in those states. Hearing that their namesakes had gone down with great loss of life, I was all the more downhearted.

A little after 11 A.M., I drove back to our bungalow for lunch. My three roommates were there, and we ate a light meal served by the Filipino staff. The lieutenant colonel was not happy to see me because of my cough, but we talked extensively about the day's events. We were certain the unprovoked attack meant full-scale war with Japan. But we all felt it would

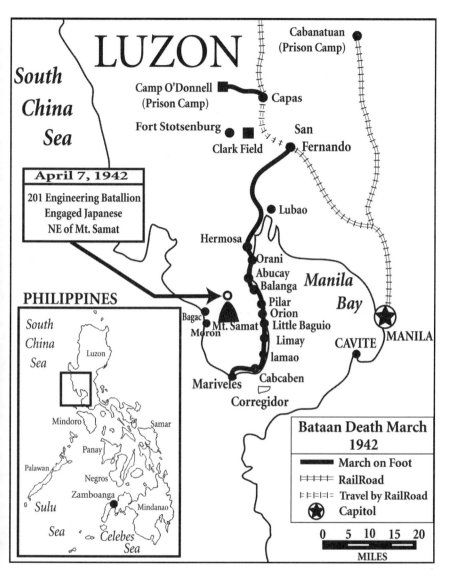

BATAAN DEATH MARCH ROUTE

be a short war and that the United States would win. The radio was on, tuned to that Manila news program. Toward the end of the meal, the announcer said, "We have an unconfirmed report that Clark Field has just been bombed." The four of us were amused by this revelation because we were sitting right in the middle of Clark Field and nothing unusual was happening. The broadcaster mentioned the unconfirmed attack several times over the next few minutes, and each time we brushed it off as an embarrassing piece of misinformation.

At one point, the adjutant lieutenant got up and walked to the back door, where he put a hand to his forehead and peered into the sky.

"See any Japs?" I asked.

"No." He laughed, as if the idea seemed ridiculous.

We were behaving nonchalantly with no sense of the severity of the situation. The adjutant lieutenant returned to the table, and dessert, a tasty pie, was served. I took two bites of my piece before the house blew up.

Seconds earlier, two flights of Japanese bombers had arrived from the western coast of the South China Sea and dumped their full complement of bombs squarely in the center of Clark Field. We had no warning. The planes had not yet appeared when the adjutant lieutenant got up to look, and we did not know they were coming until they were on top of us. For the second time that day, the Japanese caught the Americans completely by surprise.

• • •

When the bungalow exploded, it was a total shock. As the first bombs hit, the four of us jumped up and ran to an interior hallway. We covered our heads as we dove for the floor. In an instant, the adjutant lieutenant's midsection was ripped apart by shrapnel. He lay not more than a foot away from me. "I've been hit!" he cried out.

Beside the adjutant lay the major who was a doctor. The two of us picked up the injured man and headed out the back door, followed closely by the lieutenant colonel. The plumbing pipes had burst from the recoil of the bombs, spewing water everywhere, and the house was on fire. It made for a strange sight: our bungalow rapidly flooding while simultaneously burning to the ground.

We went into the backyard, where there was a foxhole. When we put down the adjutant lieutenant, the doctor realized he had forgotten his medical bag and bravely ran back through the flames to get it. I held the adjutant's head. Everywhere was smoke, noise, and confusion. Lost in the din of the attack all around us, I tried to comfort him.

"It's okay," I said. "The major's coming back, and he'll fix you right up."

For the first time, I looked at the adjutant's gaping wound. It was a ghastly sight. A fat stream of blood spewed from his abdomen, and a sizable segment of his intestines was exposed in a loose geometric pattern extending a foot or so away from his body on either side.

When the major came back, I turned to him for a sign of hope, but he shook his head in resignation. In an act of mercy, the doctor gave the adjutant a large injection of morphine to ease his suffering. I tried to offer encouragement. "Hang on, buddy. You're going to make it."

The adjutant gazed impassively at his injury without acknowledging my words. "I'm a goner," he said flatly to no one in particular, and then he died.

Afterward, things seemed to go silent, as if God had abruptly muted the tragic scene. I sat very still, numb to the world. Prior to that moment, death had never touched me directly. Now, with my friend lying lifeless in my arms, it was sickening and hard to accept.

The deafening noise of combat returned when the major's strained voice snapped me back to reality. "There's nothing I can do for him, Gene!" He yelled. "I have to go!" Before I could argue, the major jumped up and began looking for other wounded.

The lieutenant colonel and I crouched in the crater, listening to the enemy bombers deposit their murderous cargo about the base. Sunken in, we heard the confused screams of men running to and fro, frantically seeking shelter from the earth-shattering impacts. To cope with my anxiety, I studied the sound of the falling bombs, comparing it to some familiar, less menacing noise, such as dynamite being used to clear a tunnel or demolish a building. Simple mental exercises did little to quell my confusion and panic, however, and throughout the attack I felt an apprehension bordering on terror.

It seemed our location was receiving more than its share of bombing. Poking my head cautiously out of the crater, I saw why so much ordnance was falling nearby. In addition to authentic targets, the Japanese were focusing on those dummy planes, the plywood replicas of our fighters that we had purchased from the Filipinos. The decoys looked convincingly real and were parked in a neat row, like actual aircraft, across the road in front of the Bachelor Officers' Quarters (BOQ). As a result, the BOQ was hit many times and suffered great losses.

Following the initial raid, Japanese fighter planes moved in, strafing the field with machine gunfire to take care of anything the bombers missed. During the next forty-five minutes, I stared pensively up through a noxious black haze and saw swarms of silver Zero fighters pass by at treetop level. With scores of turbo-prop engines droning overhead, I slumped deeper into the crater, hoping no bullets would find me.

Many Americans fought back gallantly. The 200th Antiaircraft Unit hurled tons of artillery skyward. Soon, anyone who could man a gun was shooting at the Japanese, including me with a .45-caliber pistol, which was absurd considering how fast the planes were traveling. I might as well have grabbed some pebbles and hurled them skyward. Yet these acts of defiance showed our determination to oppose the invaders. Joining the fight also made me feel more useful, less trapped and helpless. Our resistance was only minimally effective, however. We managed to bring down just six Zeros and none of the high-flying heavy bombers that did so much damage.

• • •

After what seemed like an eternity, the Japanese strike force departed, and a siren signaled the all clear. With my ears ringing and my mind racing, I studied the gruesome remnants of Clark Field. The adjutant and all six of our servants were dead. Elsewhere, hundreds of dead and dying men, their bodies burned and bloody, lay strewn about. Many cried out desperately for help. For most, there was no relief.

The results of the initial enemy sorties were devastating. The first wave of bombers knocked out all communication facilities. In an instant, we were isolated, unable to contact Manila. The aircraft hangars and administration buildings were prime targets, and they, too, were pummeled. More ominously, the strikes destroyed our air defense capabilities. The mighty B-17s were ablaze, and pieces of the vaunted P-40 and P-35 fighters lay mangled on both runways. Only a couple of our planes got airborne during the attack, and they were quickly cut down. I saw one P-40 crash while attempting to take off. Moreover, most of our pilots, who had been at home in the BOQ, were now dead.

My thoughts turned to the safety of my workers and the condition of the runways, and I headed toward them on foot. Arriving there a few minutes later, I saw that the damage to my workplace was extensive. My office was leveled, and the construction records I had compiled over the previous five months were gone. Hundreds of impact craters, resembling lunar pockmarks, marred the field, but thankfully, there had been no casualties among my crew. Because the attack began around noon, the men were having lunch. When the first bombs fell, they wisely scurried into the revetments and were safe.

Once I assured my workers that for the moment the danger had passed, we set about restoring the runways. Additional squadrons of B-17s were due to arrive, and the landing pads had to be made usable. Most of the impact craters were relatively small, about four feet deep and eight feet wide, and readily patched with the bulldozers and graders at my disposal. (Representatives from the 803d Engineering Battalion helped with the repairs as well.) A prime advantage of earthen runways was that they were hard to damage. Holes could be knocked in them, but the holes were easily filled in and smoothed out.

My work crew and I tried to remain positive. We had confidence in the American and Filipino forces and expected reinforcements to arrive soon. Yet a mood of anxious grief had descended over Clark Field. The others must have shared my sentiment that the Japanese clearly had the upper hand now, and fighting back from this defeat would not be easy.

• • •

Several hours after the attack, I saw a friend of mine who was overseeing a burial detail, and I asked him how many people we had lost. "Sorry, Gene," he replied. "That information's classified." When I persisted, he said, "I can tell you this: We needed about four hundred blankets to wrap all the bodies in." His cryptic words explained the number killed in the initial assault on Clark Field—about four hundred.*

Just then, my buddy noticed something curious on my uniform. I raised my left arm to find that a piece of razor-sharp bomb shrapnel had penetrated the fabric beneath the armpit, without ever touching my skin. Had it gone a half-inch deeper, it might have caused permanent injury. As it was, I did not suffer a scratch. I felt fortunate and very grateful.

• • •

Most American units evacuated Clark Field at sundown on December 8. I hastily packed a duffel bag full of essentials and made camp in the nearby jungle. There was comfort in numbers, so I located the 200th Antiaircraft Unit and dug in with them for the night.

There was no moon that evening, and the darkness was unsettling. As my friends and I discussed the situation, our mood was subdued. We kept our conversation quiet. General King, the commander at Fort Stotsenburg, feared the Japanese would follow the day's attack with a paratroop drop, so the airfield was ringed with tanks from the 192d Battalion, and everyone was on full alert. I looked up nervously, searching for the open parachutes that would signal the enemy's arrival.

* Funeral services for the casualties were held within a couple of days. Enlisted men from the Quartermaster Corps had the unenviable task of identifying and burying the bodies in a temporary plot at Clark Field. One by one, dog tags were collected, graves marked, and crosses put up. A lovely cemetery was later built near Manila as a final resting place for the dead— both American and Filipino.

But paratroopers never appeared, so I just lay under the open sky, unable to sleep.

Long after midnight, I heard shouting and shooting nearby. I arose to investigate the commotion and learned that, moments earlier, an American soldier had wandered away from the camp's perimeter to go to the bathroom, and a trigger-happy sentry, assuming the man was a Japanese invader, shot and killed him. Such a tragic mishap was explainable; the aerial offensive had been terrifying, and the guards were jittery. As far as I know, it was the only friendly fire incident following the initial attack. That is surprising, considering how jumpy we all were.

• • •

Next morning, I returned to the ruins of our bungalow. The dwelling was barely recognizable, and it was hard for me to accept that, only yesterday, this burned-out shell had been our magnificent home. Gradually, my sense of loss was sinking in.

Digging through the debris, I found little of value. I salvaged some clothing, a couple of engineering manuals, and a few letters from my mother. Firefighters extinguished the flames in time to keep the external walls standing, but the ceiling had large holes in it. The place was no longer structurally sound, and I never occupied it again. Instead, I camped in various locations with the 803d. We often slept on the ground, but it was the dry season and therefore not too uncomfortable. I am not sure what happened to my two surviving housemates. I never saw either of them again.

Later, I listened to a radio broadcast that featured a discussion of President Roosevelt's address to Congress, in which he asked for a formal declaration of war against Japan. The speech was inspiring, and the men stationed in the Philippines took his words to heart. Stirred by his call to arms, we dug in and vowed to hold our position. (Three days later, on December 11, Germany declared war on the United States, bringing America into the European conflict as well.)

After the first bombing, many Filipino civilians left their jobs at Clark Field, including some who worked for me. I had no authority to make them stay and understood their not wanting to continue in harm's way. Most of my employees kept their jobs, however, and dutifully showed up the next morning. One of the contractors asked me to get the men military helmets for protection. Determined not to lose good help, I went immediately to Fort Stotsenburg and requested the headgear from the quartermaster, who willingly obliged. The appreciative Filipinos stayed with me and kept up with construction for the next three weeks. I admired their loyalty. Given proper training, they would have made fine soldiers.

My crew's next order of business was to pull the remaining wooden dummy planes to the far end of the runways—away from crucial structures. We threw tree branches over the decoys to make them look like real planes that we were trying to camouflage. Our trick worked; the Japanese hit the fake planes many times. After each attack, we moved them to another safe spot, threw more brush over them, and dared the enemy to hit them again. It became a game of cat-and-mouse. Deception was the only ploy we had, and we succeeded in drawing a few shells away from the actual targets. From December 8 through the 23, the Japanese bombed Clark Field every day around noon. Since they had destroyed everything of importance on the first day, the subsequent onslaught produced little damage. General Jonathan Wainwright, commander of the I Philippine Corps, immediately sent round-the-clock observation crews into the mountains northwest of the base. The lookouts signaled whenever enemy bombers were approaching. With advance warning, we suffered few additional casualties.

During an attack the sirens sounded, and everyone fled to the abundant zigzag trenches that had been dug throughout the base by details of enlisted men. (The trenches were about three feet wide and four feet deep and were dug in a Z-like pattern every ten feet or so. This angled shape limited injuries from flying shrapnel when shells landed nearby.) Construction of the trenches had begun several weeks earlier, but until December 8, the diggers had shown little enthusiasm. Frequently seen resting on their shovels, they talked much and dug little. When the war started, however, those men found their motivation and soon dug so many trenches that you could hardly take two steps in any direction without falling into one.

By late December we had become so used to the regular air raids that taking shelter became a casual routine. If two men were having a discussion when an attack began, they would continue it without interruption underground, the bombs landing close by. Gone was the panicked exhilaration of the first day. I thought the Japanese wasted a lot of ordnance that month. But the constant bombardment was demoralizing and slowly wore us down. It also destroyed the airfield. When we were not ducking bombs, my men and I waged an uphill battle to patch the runways, which ultimately mattered little, since we had few planes left.

• • •

With American tanks encircling Clark Field, the Japanese massed troops on board ship in the South China Sea and prepared for an amphibious assault. On December 19, they landed at Lingayen Gulf, one hundred miles north of Clark Field, with a contingent so powerful that our forces had little hope of resisting it. General MacArthur sent Filipino units, including the vaunted 26th Cavalry, to oppose the Japanese, but their planes and tanks shredded our regiments. Quickly retreating, our men fought a delaying action back toward central Luzon.

Additional Japanese forces landed south of Manila, and several Filipino divisions fought futilely to slow their advance on that front, too. News of the invasion was very disturbing. Having established a beachhead, I knew the Japanese were on the islands to stay. Clark Field was a prime objective, and they would reach it within days.

As it turned out, one of the few structures to survive the intensified aerial onslaught was a big building located at the edge of Clark Field. Nicknamed "The Barn," it served as a temporary headquarters for the 803d Battalion. On December 22, I had Christmas dinner there. It was splendid with turkey, dressing, fruit, and candy, and was the last sumptuous meal I would eat for four years. But it was not a festive time for any of us. The faces around me were grim.

Reinforcing our sense of dread were administrative officers who advised everyone at the party to enroll in a supplemental life insurance program offered by the government. Due to the circumstances, the army was recommending that each soldier purchase $10,000 of coverage at a nominal rate. Almost everyone signed up for the added indemnity, although some families of those lost never received compensation because the policies were destroyed before they could be sent to the War Department for processing. I, for one, was never able to convince Washington that I had in fact signed up for the added insurance.

Throughout the day, chaplains ministered to our religious needs. They led us in hymns; offered eloquent, thoughtful prayers; and made it as true a Christmas in the spiritual sense as possible. Their efforts were fruitful, and many men accepted Christ that day. I spent time in prayer, but, as is my way, I did it privately and on my own terms.

While the holiday remained sacred to us, it was just another afternoon of conquest for the Japanese. Right on schedule, their planes came over and bombed the base. I walked to the open doors of the barn and observed shells exploding in spectacular, if predictable, fashion near the terminal area, half a mile away. In no real danger, I watched the attack for a while. When I turned to finish eating, a friend observed, "The Japs really are a bunch of party-poopers, aren't they."

I laughed at the childlike innocence of his statement. But he was right. We were merely going through the motions of revelry. We realized that, very soon, we would have to evacuate Clark Field. Enemy divisions were closing in on us quickly, and there was no alternative if we hoped to survive.

Since I could not change the situation, I decided to focus on happier thoughts. By nightfall, I was recalling peaceful Christmases surrounded by family and friends back home—memories made extra special in comparison to this grim day. Before falling asleep, I prayed earnestly that I might be allowed to enjoy another Christmas.

• • •

On Christmas Eve, the 803d Engineering Battalion was ordered to evacuate Clark Field and move to the southern peninsula of Bataan. Knowing that construction engineers would be needed in advance of the other troops, Major Fischer instructed me to gather as much equipment as I could and go at the same time.

I assembled my crews to explain the situation. "Fellas," I said. "We can no longer hold the field. It's time to bug out. Who will come with me to Bataan?"

I had no takers among the contractors. Older, affluent men with no particular beef against the Japanese, they were content to sit out the war at home. I did convince about thirty of the civilian workers to go with me, on condition that I would get each of them a rifle. "No problem," I said, and hurried to Fort Stotsenburg to procure the guns from the quartermaster.

The weapons were World War I vintage Springfields and Enfields. I felt embarrassed to offer the men such inferior arms, but there was no choice. They were the best rifles we had.

Weapons in hand, we went to the rail depot at Angeles. I wasted no time commandeering several empty flatcars, which my men began loading with our equipment. Other departing units also filled the train with machinery, and it became a prime transport for the trip to Bataan. There was a large warehouse that belonged to the Filipino Public Works Agency located on the banks of the nearby Pampanga River. It was full of construction hardware, including some valuable spare parts I knew we would need. So, on the authority of the army, I attempted to seize it. Naturally, the Filipino officials were not happy about this, and I hurriedly signed documents promising reimbursment later. I was putting them in an awkward position but felt certain the U.S. government would compensate them in full—even if I were not around to vouch for my deeds.*

* The Americans did follow up on the matter. Years after the war, I received a letter from the State Department inquiring as to the whereabouts of that train I took charge of. I replied that I had no idea where it was and suggested they ask the Japanese.

With the train fully loaded, our caravan departed for San Fernando, about sixty miles away. I followed as closely as possible in one of our trucks, also packed with construction implements. The journey took a full day because bumper-to-bumper traffic slowed us to a crawl. Everyone was nervous, fearing an assault by Japanese fighters, and we were relieved to arrive without being attacked.

· · ·

We reached the railhead at San Fernando on Christmas Day, unloaded our equipment, and then started south down a gravel road along the coast. A few miles away, the road converged with the main highway from Manila and continued south through Bataan, ending at the town of Mariveles. During the retreat, our forces were doing all they could on both fronts to slow the enemy advance. The Japanese had breached our beach-front defenses, so the only hope was to fall back, entrench ourselves, and attempt to deny them control of Manila Bay for as long as possible.

The highway was jam-packed with thousands of vehicles. The approximately eighty thousand troops moving into Bataan during a ten-day period could have been a logistical nightmare. But those were professional army units with competent leaders, and it was an orderly, disciplined retreat. That the mammoth operation was so tidy is a tribute to the efficiency of the U.S. Army.

The psychological value of our accomplishment cannot be overstated. The successful retreat into Bataan demonstrated how capable we were of adapting to any contingency, fully resolved to fight on.

My men and I traveled slowly until we reached a small stream about thirty miles from the southern tip of Bataan, where we made camp. We were among the first troops—mostly service units, such as the 803d Engineers, the Quartermaster Corps, and the ordnance people—who arrived in Bataan to set up while the others continued streaming in.

I lost touch with Major Fischer and could not reach him. So I quickly contacted Major Clarence Bidgood, the commander of the 803d, who issued my orders from then on. Bataan, our base of operations for the foreseeable future, was being organized into two corps along the eastern and western sides of the peninsula. All were still under the central authority of General MacArthur, who had moved his headquarters to the island of Corregidor.

Bataan was mountainous and heavily forested. There were few clearings and trails and just the one road along the east coast of the peninsula. Rivers and streams were plentiful, but bridges were not. Developing infrastructure was a top priority, and the engineering units were put to work building the roads and other structures needed to make that rugged land support a functioning army of some eighty thousand men. On the day after Christmas 1941, my mission as a construction engineer in the Philippines began its most urgent and important phase.

CHAPTER 4

WE SHALL REMAIN

With the evacuation into Bataan complete, our leaders positioned troops strategically around the peninsula. The mountainous terrain made it difficult to attack us directly through the center of Bataan, so most of our artillery was concentrated in the coastal flatlands along the main highway, where top brass thought the Japanese would strike en masse. The 192d and the 194th tank battalions were sent to the east side of Bataan, but their tanks had limited mobility, and in the course of the later conflict they were reduced to semimobile artillery pieces.

The bulk of our ground forces, including three Filipino regiments (the 26th Cavalry and the 45th and the 57th Infantries) and the only American infantry unit in the Philippines, the 31st Regiment, dug in along a twenty-mile line halfway across the peninsula from Abucay to Moron. Artillery batteries were positioned behind these regiments, and Air Corps personnel were issued weapons and sent to reinforce them.

The 200th Antiaircraft unit took up position at the southern end of Bataan to defend headquarters and our supplies, which were stored in the surrounding jungle. The 803d Engineering Battalion was building two airstrips in case reserves could be flown in, and we positioned antiaircraft guns there to defend the runways. Finally, marines from the 4th Regiment were sent to Mariveles, the southernmost point on Luzon Island, to guard its port. With our forces properly deployed, we dug in to await the Japanese. Although conditions were harsher than in Manila, morale remained high and we believed we would win in the end.

•   •   •

A month later, I was ordered by Major Bidgood to join the 201st Engineering Battalion, a group of inadequately trained and poorly armed Filipino draftees commanded by Harry Fischer, my former supervisor at Clark Field. At that point, Major Bidgood took control of the laborers and equipment that I had brought from Clark Field. I thanked my men for their devotion and wished them good luck. They were then sent to work at different areas on the peninsula, and we never met again. I do not know what happened to most of them, but judging from the shocking number of casualties the islanders suffered, I fear that many did not survive the fighting.*

* After the war, I received letters from three of the Filipinos who had worked for me. They were trying to verify that they had served at Bataan in order to receive payment from the U.S. government. Unfortunately, I did not remember the men by name, but I believed their claims and felt they were entitled to compensation, and I wrote to the War Department on their behalf.

My new company of "combat engineers" consisted of some two hundred peasants who could not do much except perform manual labor. They worked hard, however, building roads and trails along the east coast of Bataan to support the communication, supply, and logistics needs of our forces. I was not the only one with an unproven crew. More than half of the soldiers holed up at Bataan were raw Filipino recruits. American officers attempted to train these men, but not very successfully. Our unit got a needed infusion of talent when some of the civilians who accompanied U.S. forces to Bataan enlisted in the army. Not only were these new officers capable engineers, they spoke the regional dialects and had experience supervising Filipino laborers, which helped make up for their lack of military background. With few exceptions, they were bright men who served with distinction.

In contrast to our unpolished outfits, the Japanese launched against us a force of forty thousand well-trained men. They were crack troops, veterans of years of fighting against the Chinese. After they destroyed our planes at Clark Field on December 8, the Japanese controlled the skies, and they used their warships to blockade Luzon Island and cut off our supply lines.

Our backs were to the wall, but we had advantages. We greatly increased the range of our artillery by positioning it high in the mountains—something the enemy could not do—and because we fought a purely defensive effort anything short of surrender meant victory. That required far fewer resources than an invasion did. In the beginning, I felt we had a good chance of holding out against the Japanese. Still, had the siege been a poker game, I would rather have played the enemy's hand.

• • •

The Japanese attacked the American line on January 9, 1942. One Japanese regiment broke through but was stopped by the Philippine Army, which cut them off and encircled them. Isolated from their comrades, the Japanese regiment held out for a week. They refused to surrender and were all killed. While encouraging, this victory demonstrated the fanatical determination of imperial soldiers. The Japanese also landed several thousand men on the east coast of Bataan. There, high cliffs and heavy jungle slowed their progress, and eventually a Filipino division wiped them out. We estimated they lost more than eight thousand soldiers in both battles.

Following these defeats, the Japanese launched no concerted attacks for several weeks as they regrouped and brought in reinforcements from Singapore. The initial setbacks surprised the Japanese, who did not expect us to put up much of a fight. They anticipated conquering the Philippines in about a month. Instead, it took them *four* months. The delay proved fatal to their subsequent plans of quickly invading Guadalcanal and Australia, and their failure to gain control of those strategic locations cost them later in the war. Our dogged resistance at Bataan diminished their prospects for victory in the Pacific. For that, the emperor's army was determined to make us pay dearly.

• • •

When fighting broke out on the front lines, I was still assigned to the rear, building roads along the coast, but in our spare time, my men and I did what we could to aid the defense effort. Our tactics resembled guerrilla warfare. For instance, there were several farms in the area ringed with barbed-wire fences, and we tore them down and gave the barbed wire to the infantry to erect near the front to impede the Japanese advance. Other support units helped out, too. One night some engineers hauled a thousand-pound antiship mine to the front and buried it in an area where the Japanese had concentrated ground troops. Those who survived the blast were no doubt very jittery afterward.

Other engineers manufactured antipersonnel mines. Someone devised a way to make them out of bamboo shells filled with dynamite. They inserted nails to create shrapnel, and detonating devices were activated when the mines were stepped on. These crude weapons were potent but tricky to build, and several American soldiers were maimed while producing them.

Throughout the standoff, American forces were under constant threat from Japanese planes. The danger was great. Japanese planes could appear overhead in seconds, and I kept an eye out for a bunker to jump into if they entered my area. The Zeros usually attacked in a triangular configuration of three planes. If they turned toward you and started into a glide, you knew to flee and hit the ground if you wanted to live. Initially, we Americans were well hidden in the dense jungles, but over time, with so many people and vehicles moving about, paths were worn in and our positions exposed, making us easy targets for aerial bombing. Still, we were committed to resisting the Japanese Air Force and used the natural resources of Bataan to maximum benefit. Banyan trees, which have large, solid roots four to five inches thick that extend from their branches to the ground like multiple trunks, grew there and made for good cover when the Zeros came on strafing runs. We took shelter in the banyan trees on numerous occasions. Hiding inside them, one of us thought what a logical place they would be to house extra artillery placements—if we had any to spare.

Then someone else had an idea. Taking logs from an abandoned timber mill, our men painted them black, elevated them on sawhorses, and placed them under the banyan trees. With their dark ends sticking out and pointing upward they looked like cannon barrels and made nice targets for the incessantly circling planes.

When a group of Zeros passed overhead, we ignited sticks of dynamite to produce a loud boom and send up clouds of dust and smoke, as if an artillery shell had just been fired. Then we ran out the back of the trees and got as far away from them as we could. (I could be a hundred yards away in seconds!) Thinking they had located artillery, the enemy planes turned quickly and bore down on our position, releasing their bombs and firing at our hidden "installation." When they left, we would return to collect the painted logs, move them to other banyan trees, and wait to repeat the sting. This practice was dangerous, but we were willing to do anything to draw enemy ordnance, because that left them with fewer bombs to use against our real defenses.

During that time, I greatly enjoyed tuning into the Tokyo radio stations that broadcast anti-American propaganda in English every night. In an effort to demoralize us, they announced the number of artillery pieces that Japanese fighters had destroyed on Bataan that day. My men and I listened with amusement, knowing that some of them were in fact our wooden fakes. Outsmarting the empire in such a simple manner gave us a tremendous lift. We engaged in the banyan-tree deception numerous times over several weeks before the Japanese caught on. It was bound to happen, with no shells exploding along with the dynamite blasts. They stopped bombing our wooden artillery pieces, and we decided not to waste any more time placing them. But our trick was fun while it lasted.

Japanese propaganda was ineffective because none of us took it seriously. Over the airwaves, a kind voice offered "good treatment" if we surrendered immediately. Yeah, right, we thought. We knew how they treated the Chinese who surrendered at Nanking—promising mercy only to renege on it in the most horrific way. We felt their similar offer to us was ludicrous, an insult to our intelligence. The Japanese also dropped pamphlets urging us to give up. The leaflets claimed, among other things, that our wives and sweethearts were having "great pleasure" back home with other men. We genuinely appreciated these pages because there was a real shortage of toilet paper at Bataan.

• • •

During the siege of Bataan, our fatal weakness was a shortage of food. With no way to get supplies in, we had only the provisions we brought with us from Manila. When they were gone, there would be nothing left to eat. Rice was the staple of our diet, and it was rationed from the day we left Clark Field. With more than one hundred thousand soldiers and civilians to feed, however, the rice soon began to run out. Thousands of bushels of grain were warehoused in central Luzon, but none of it was taken to Bataan. In the haste to evacuate, our leaders left it behind, even though there was time to load much of it onto the hundreds of trucks that arrived in Bataan *empty*. That extra rice would have fed our army for weeks—possibly enabling us to delay the Japanese conquest of the Philippines indefinitely. But because of poor planning, it was not to be. Instead, the Japanese, who had to import much of their rice, seized a bonanza.

Before surrendering, we did what we could to satisfy our hunger. American scouts located small farms and plantations, which helped feed us for a while. Their efforts were hampered initially by some idiotic restrictions on what animals we could kill for food. The barrios of Bataan, for example, teemed with the meaty carabao—just one of them could feed an entire company—but the carabao were the lifeblood of the Filipino agricultural economy (the farmers depended on them to pull their plows), and General MacArthur ordered us not to shoot them. It seemed insane. We were being starved into submission, and MacArthur was worried about us causing hardship on the civilians by treating ourselves to a few of the numerous beasts. More amazingly, his order was largely obeyed throughout the winter, although there were subtle ways around it. Occasionally we found a sick or wounded specimen, which we quickly "put out of its misery." But those opportunities were few. By the last days of the siege, MacArthur's edict was totally disobeyed as ravenous Americans shot any carabao, healthy or otherwise, on sight.

The 201st Engineering Battalion also assigned troops to scour the jungle for food. At first, they were able to find creatures like birds and lizards to keep us alive, but as time passed, those populations became depleted. The patrols then started producing odd foods that were often unidentifiable. Nobody cared what they brought back as long as it was edible, and few dared to ask what they were throwing into the pot for each night's dinner.

As our work intensified, my men and I became hungrier and also got into the act. Once, when we were staking out a road in the jungle, a soldier spotted an enormous snake (probably a python), some twenty feet long and as thick as a man's leg, lying on a log just ahead of us. Wanting that monstrous reptile for lunch, we drew our guns and machetes. But in our excitement, we frightened the snake, causing it to slither away into the vegetation. My men searched frantically, but could not find it again. That was heartbreaking, since we could have eaten that snake for a week. Instead, we continued on, empty-handed and famished.

About a month into the siege, our daily food allotments were cut in half for the second time. This reduced us to starvation rations. The men rapidly lost weight and became susceptible to diseases such as dysentery and malaria. As we ran out of medical supplies, more and more men were unable to function. By spring about half of the soldiers of the 201st were incapacitated, literally too sick and hungry to get up. That ultimately led to our defeat; the Japanese overran us after most of our men were physically unable to continue fighting.

• • •

In early 1942, haggard yet confident, most Americans trapped at Bataan still believed that their leaders would send reinforcements. Few realized how critical the situation was, how completely the Japanese blockade had isolated us from the rest of the Pacific command. By relentless pressure, the emperor's land, air, and sea forces were eroding our defenses, taking away our ability to protect ourselves. The senior officers must have known that all was lost after the annihilation of our air force at Clark Field. Because they never shared those feelings, we carried on against overwhelming odds much longer than we would have otherwise.

I certainly did not think things were hopeless. General MacArthur reassured us regularly that help was on the way, if we just held fast. But with things turning desperate, he would soon flee Bataan, leaving behind an army without hope against an imperial war machine.

• • •

The propaganda leaflets that the Japanese dropped over Bataan on March 12 contained true information, facts they must have loved sharing with us. General MacArthur had secretly fled the Philippines the night before, taking refuge in the relative safety of Australia.

Knowing how the Japanese often spread lies to demoralize us, a lot of men initially refused to believe the news. "That's crazy," someone said, ripping one of the papers in half. "General MacArthur would never leave like that."

The fact that MacArthur still had ardent defenders seems amazing now, considering his rather detached way of handling things. For the previous ten weeks, the general had lived securely underground at Corregidor, eating well and issuing increasingly wooden words of encouragement to those of us trapped in the line of fire. Many men no longer respected him. But while displaying contempt for MacArthur the man, most soldiers still had faith in him as a commander. That was why they were shocked by the radio reports confirming that he was gone.

In the early morning hours of March 11, acting on orders from President Roosevelt, General MacArthur, his family and staff, and the president and first lady of the Philippines fled Corregidor by PT boat for the island of Mindanao. There they transferred to two B–17 Flying Fortresses that flew the entourage to the city of Darwin, in northern Australia. From Darwin, MacArthur issued the signature statement of his career: "The President of the United States ordered me to break through the Japanese lines and proceed from Corregidor to Australia for the purpose, as I understand, of organizing the American offensive against Japan, a primary purpose of which is the relief of the Philippines. I came through and I shall return."*

* Quoted in C.L. Sulzberger, *The American Heritage Picture History of World War II* (New York : American Heritage Pub. Co., 1966), p. 148.

MacArthur claimed that his departure was necessary for the long-term good of the war effort. He also tried to motivate us to fight on in his absence. But reaction to his address was mixed. Some men who liked MacArthur took comfort in his words. Others were angry that he sneaked out the way he did.

"I guess *we shall remain,*" someone commented in a play on MacArthur's words. "Until we finally get our asses shot off!" "The son of a bitch ran out," another decried. "Unbelievable."

Virtually everyone I talked to was discouraged by MacArthur's exodus, but I thought he was right to flee when he did. As much as I now disliked MacArthur, I understood that the president needed to be able to tap his considerable experience later in the war. To allow the Japanese to capture the supreme commander of American Forces in the Far East would have been a huge blow to morale on the home front. So, for the good of the war effort, I was glad MacArthur got safely out of Bataan. If only there was a way out for the rest of us.

• • •

As discouraged as we were after March 12, life went on. I had orders to build some barracks before the upcoming rainy season, and I urged my crews to complete the job on time. Having work to keep us busy did little to lift our spirits, however. The work was backbreaking and we were in bad shape physically. I now weighed less than one hundred pounds. Everyone else was weakened by loss of weight, and we worked inefficiently. We did not finish the barracks before Bataan fell.

The men of Bataan were becoming desperate. One day in late March, our battalion's supply officer told me that he had tried to get us something to eat, but all that was left was seven jars of mustard. Racked by weeks of deadly combat, the elite Filipino Scouts soon arrived back at headquarters. Starving, they butchered their horses for food. It was an inglorious but inevitable end to one of the proudest equestrian units ever to serve in the U.S. Army.

Anticipation of rescue gone, we now realized that our fate had been sealed at Pearl Harbor. The navy's crippled Far East Fleet would not recover for at least a year, and its remaining ships were sent to protect Australia. Nothing could be done to save those of us trapped in the Philippines, and no resources would be wasted in a futile effort.

Under MacArthur's successor, General Wainwright, we struggled on. Robbed of hope, someone composed a song that bluntly summarized our attitude. In part, it went:

> "We're the battling bastards of Bataan;
> No mamma, no pappa, no Uncle Sam;
> No aunts, no uncles, no nephews, no nieces;
> No pills, no planes, no artillery pieces.
> . . . and nobody gives a damn!*

As sorrow gripped the ranks, men entertained fantastic thoughts, and wild rumors spread across the peninsula. For example, we had a few P-40 fighters left, which the Air Corps kept hidden. Once in a while they would make a quick reconnaissance over the area to report on Japanese troop activity. These flights were risky, and headquarters never announced them beforehand. When men on the ground saw American planes overhead, they thought reinforcements had arrived and their hearts soared. But when reality hit them, they felt even sadder than before. Some of them would not speak to anyone for days afterward.

By late March the Japanese understood that we were near the end and increased their activities tremendously. More and

* Sulzberger, *American Heritage Picture History of World War II*, p. 148.

more planes bombed the peninsula. From a ridge overlooking Manila Bay, we saw dozens of Japanese aircraft blast Corregidor mercilessly. Such assaults came several times a day for more than a week, and the death toll mounted. It was the final, overwhelming push.

• • •

During the last days of March, around the time of my twenty-fifth birthday, I helped capture an enemy spy. I had gone with my Filipino driver to Mariveles to request additional fuel for our construction equipment, as well as to visit friends in the 803d Engineering Battalion. Late that evening we headed back to camp on one of the roads my men were building. The course was still very rough, and at the top of a ridge we had to stop, park the jeep for fear of damaging it, and continue the rest of the way on foot.

As the two of us walked, we kept our voices low in case there were enemy scouts nearby. It was a beautiful starry night, and as we approached camp, we paused for a moment to view the magnificent panorama of the bay below. A one-ton army truck with a canvas cover over its bed was parked about a hundred yards away.

Suddenly, the flare of a Roman candle shot into the air. As it exploded in a flash of brilliant light, the driver and I looked at each other. Tracing the projectile's path, we deduced that it had been launched from the rear of that truck, so we ran down there immediately. At first we saw no one. I had a flashlight and shined it cautiously into the truck bed. Hiding in a corner was a small man dressed in civilian clothes. I heard the Filipino, who was armed with a rifle, throw a bullet into its chamber. I then drew my pistol.

"He looks Japanese," my driver said. "Are you sure?" I asked. At that time I could not tell a Japanese person from a Filipino. To me, the man could be a local farmer. Later, during my years in Japan, I learned to distinguish between the two races, one being Asian and the other Polynesian.

I ordered the man out of the truck, and he complied without resistance. The driver then questioned him in Tagalog, their common language, and said he was Japanese. The prisoner was uncooperative. He volunteered no information and answered tersely the questions put to him, so I tied his hands behind his back. The commotion had aroused some Filipino soldiers, who appeared on the scene, and I sent one of them in my jeep back onto the main road to find MPs. In the meantime, I guarded the man carefully. I had to remain focused and in control because the gathering crowd wanted to kill him.

About thirty minutes later, the soldier I sent up the road returned with a group of MPs. I explained what had happened, and they wrote a report, which I signed, and then took the prisoner away. I do not know what happened to the spy after that, whether he was executed, or whether the Japanese rescued him before he could be tried.

Many Japanese citizens lived in the Philippines at the time of the war. Most remained loyal to Emperor Hirohito and a sizable number served as saboteurs. A common trick for these agents was to approach a military garrison at night and set off Roman candles to help Japanese observers pinpoint the location. This practice seemed futile to me. I would see these rockets in the darkness and realize that someone was attempting to signal Japanese units who were at least several miles away and could not see the fireworks. My men and I tried to laugh off such amateurish tactics, but it was unsettling to know that enemy sympathizers were all around, trying to harm us. It made me look over my shoulder, and as the Japanese grew stronger, the nighttime jungle seemed to close in menacingly.

Civilian Conservation Corps enrollees with tools of their trade—books for attending the university in the morning and picks and shovels for building roads the rest of the day. Gene Boyt is on the right. Courtesy of Gene Boyt.

Gene Boyt on graduating from the Missouri School of Mines in 1941.
Courtesy of Gene Boyt.

From left to right: Gene Boyt, Lieutenant Jack McAnerny, and Bob Silhavy on arrival in Manila aboard the *President Cleveland* in July 1941. McAnerny, who was also a new graduate of the Missouri School of Mines, was killed less than a year later during the siege of Corregidor. Courtesy of Gene Boyt.

In "The Bombing of Clark Field," Ben Steele captures the devastation wrought by the surprise Japanese attack conducted only hours after the attack on Pearl Harbor. Courtesy of Ben Steele.

"Beginning the March." This painting by Ben Steele illustrates the anguish of American prisoners fearing for their lives at the hands of brutal Japanese guards. They have just bayoneted an unfortunate American too weak to undertake the Death March. Steele was a Bataan survivor and is now professor of art emeritus at the University of Montana–Billings. Courtesy of Ben Steele.

Filipino Scouts display a captured Japanese sword. U.S. Army Signal Corps photo.

An American prisoner is surrounded by Japanese guards during the Bataan Death March. U.S. Army Signal Corps photo.

Parts of Manila burn during a Japanese air raid.
U.S. Army Signal Corps photo.

Japanese troops move south toward Bataan in January 1942. U.S. Army Signal Corps photo.

An American prisoner is interrogated by Japanese soldiers during the
Death March. U.S. Army Signal Corps photo.

American and Philippine troops surrender at Corregidor, May 6, 1942.
Courtesy of National Archives, photo no. WEC#1142.

These prisoners were forced to endure the Bataan Death March with their hands tied behind their backs. Courtesy of National Archives, photo no. WEC#1144.

American POWs at Camp O'Donnell use makeshift litters to carry their fallen comrades for burial. Courtesy of National Archives, photo no. WEC.#1145.

Roko Roshi, September 1945. Former POWs eat from food packages dropped by U.S. aircraft. Courtesy of National Archives, photo no. 111-SC-212146-5.

Former POWs at Roko Roshi inspecting the provisions dropped to them by Army Air Corps personnel in September 1945. The backside of the barracks had a hole in the roof caused when a food barrel fell through it. Courtesy of National Archives, photo no. 111-SC-212143-3.

A closer view of former POWs at Camp Roko Roshi inspecting some food dropped by parachute from American planes following the Japanese surrender. Courtesy of National Archives, photo no. 111-SC-212144-5.

Former POWs at Roko Roshi thanking one of the American nurses who accompanied the First Cavalry on the mission to rescue them. Courtesy of National Archives, photo no. 111-SC-223947.

The former POWs at Roko Roshi assemble for the first time under their own command following the Japanese surrender. Courtesy of National Archives, Photo no. 111-SC-224004.

Gene Boyt (left) shaking hands with the lieutenant who led the First Cavalry unit that rescued the POWs from Camp Roko Roshi, September 1945. Courtesy of National Archives, photo no. 111-SC-223949.

Boyt's friend, Jim Baldwin, stands first in line, waiting to be interviewed by the U.S. Army nurses who accompanied the rescuing First Cavalry Battallion. Courtesy of National Archives, photo no. 111-SC-222981.

General Douglas MacArthur, supreme commander of Allied Forces, is photographed at the Atsugi Air Drome near Tokyo on August 30, 1945. Courtesy of National Archives, photo no. 208-PU-125J-11.

Gene Boyt, left, with Bob Silhavy shortly after the war. Courtesy of Gene Boyt.

Betty Ruth and Gene Boyt in June of 1946, shortly after their May wedding. Courtesy of Gene Boyt.

Gene Boyt (in white shirt) posing with a Philippine soldier at a ceremony in Manila commemorating the forty-fifth anniversary of the fall of the Philippines, May 1987. Courtesy of Gene Boyt.

Gene Boyt (wearing sunglasses) shaking hands with S. Laurel, then the vice president and later president of the Philippines, at the ceremony commemorating the forty-fifth anniversary of the fall of the Philippines. Courtesy of Gene Boyt.

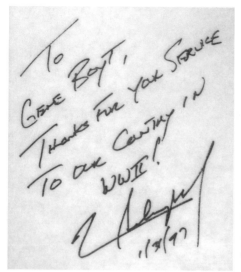

An autograph with thanks from General Norman Schwarzkopf. Courtesy of Gene Boyt.

Betty Ruth and Gene Boyt with their four grandchildren. From left to right: Tom's daughters Abbie, Kami, and Shoni; Gene and Betty Ruth; and Robert's son, Brandon. The occasion was the Boyts' fiftieth wedding anniversary on May 30, 1996. Courtesy of Gene Boyt.

CHAPTER 5

"I MIGHT AS WELL SURENDER, TOO"

On April 3, the Japanese launched a decisive assault on the American forces defending Bataan. The main thrust was in the east, against the forces of the II Corps. Two days later my 201st Battalion was ordered to the front. I will never forget how the orders read: we were to proceed to a point just to the right of the 57th Filipino Scouts and to the left of the 31st Infantry. Well, an entire Philippine *division*, consisting of about twenty thousand soldiers, had held that spot until the Japanese overran it. Now the 201st, reduced by disease and starvation to about one hundred men, was stepping in. Somehow we were expected to plug that giant hole in our defenses!

It seemed a doomed mission, and it was the low point for me—the moment I truly felt I would not make it through the war. I did not resent being sent into battle, for I was spared that duty longer than most, but I just could not see how our badly depleted unit could accomplish anything—except get a lot of people killed.

"Men," I announced, "we're going to the front." I explained that the II Corps had fallen back several miles, and if the Japanese were allowed to move much closer, their artillery would be in range of Corregidor, which would be the end of us all. "So you must hold that line at all cost."

I could tell from the rumbling murmurs that the news was not well received among the Filipinos. They were scared. Sensing that things were hopeless, they could not see sacrificing themselves to a lost cause. I could not either, but it was not my decision to make, so to the front lines we would go.

• • •

Major Fischer ordered us to move out that night. Unknown to me, our battalion had some extra rice saved from the daily rations. Before leaving we broke it out and gave everybody one final, hearty meal—the last meal for many. Afterward, we loaded our weapons, mainly bolt-action Enfield rifles, into trucks and started north up one of the newly constructed roads. I took a long look back, in case I never saw camp again. Settled on the truck, I envisioned what lay ahead when we reached our destination.

Early in the trip, one of the other young officers approached me. "Gene, do you think we can hold that line?" I was skeptical but wanted to sound encouraging. "There is always a chance," I replied. My words were hardly a ringing endorsement. Yet they seemed to elevate the man's spirits. He smiled, and went back to the other end of the truck. It felt good to boost his sagging confidence. If only someone could have boosted mine.

We drove on through the darkness, turning onto a rugged path winding through the high mountains in the center of Bataan. Around 9:30 A.M. we reached the end of the trail. There, we unloaded our gear and hiked into the jungle toward the front lines. An officer from the 57th Infantry, Major John Olson, led our unit several miles to the spot where his regiment was engaging the Japanese. We heard the explosive sounds of combat growing louder as we drew closer to the heart of battle. My adrenaline level peaked, and I thought I was going to die.

In the commotion of the war zone, odd things happened. Several of us got lost at the front and ended up about two miles *ahead* of the Fifty-seventh Regiment. Luckily, we did not encounter resistance until we came to the top of a ridge overlooking a small creek, which we had to cross before climbing a steeper crest on the other side. No sooner did I get to the top of the second ridge than firing broke out behind me. The men in the rear of the battalion came running up. Some of them were wounded and bleeding.

"What happened?" I asked. "The Japs were waiting to ambush us as we crossed the creek!" came the reply.

At that point, things got very confusing. The initial firing stopped, and I stood still without making a sound. I could hear Japanese soldiers talking all around me. Apparently, the enemy had driven even deeper into our territory than we realized. When a Japanese soldier spotted us seconds later, they opened fire again.

I quickly ducked behind a bamboo fence, held my rifle over its top, and returned fire. As the bullets flew by, it occurred to me that hollow bamboo offered scant protection. So I took refuge behind a large tree. Some of my comrades were shooting too, and the fighting continued for quite a while. Pinned down in the center of the battle, I heard many screams and shouts, including the final cries of those killed by bullets that found their mark.

I saw mortar fire landing at least two miles to our rear. The Japanese artillery hit the spot where we had unloaded from the trucks. As far as I could tell, they had killed the remaining American personnel in the area. We were obviously way too close to the Japanese, who were closing in on us. As the Japanese continued to attack along the front line, mortar shells landed near us. My men and I were sitting ducks and about to become dead ones.

Someone had to take action if we were going to survive. I knew that our battalion headquarters was about a quarter-mile to the west and thought we should go there to consolidate our forces. I tried to set up a formation to travel, but the Filipinos near me did not know what to do. They panicked, and since most of them did not speak English, I could not communicate my orders to them. Just when things looked hopeless, a lieutenant named Warren Remsnyder, who happened to be from Oklahoma City, stepped up.

"Our only chance is to rejoin our headquarters platoon!" I yelled. "You're right," he replied. "Let's go."

The two of us convinced the Filipinos to follow us through the explosive firefight, and we brought them several hundred yards up to where the battalion platoon was located. At the top of the ridge, we regrouped with Major Fischer. After conferring with us, he decided that we should all retreat to the south. The major attempted to organize everyone. But the command was dissolving. We had lost most of our Filipino troops. They simply bolted out of the ranks and hid in the jungle. A lot of the draftees had civilian clothes in their packs, and the minute they got out of sight, they put them on. If they encountered Japanese soldiers, they would try to convince them that they were merely farmers not involved in the fighting. I could not blame the Filipinos for deserting. Under the circumstances, I might have done the same thing, although I am sure that the Japanese killed many of them anyway.

• • •

Later in the day, after we started south, Major Fischer told us, "Fellas, we've got to regroup at corps headquarters." Because everything was so chaotic, we would not try to maintain a formation. "It'll be every man for himself," he said. "Get to headquarters, and we'll regroup there."

With that, the major wished us good luck and sent us on our way. A number of the remaining soldiers attached themselves to me, and we started south down the trail toward Mariveles. Just then detachments of the Philippine Scouts passed us as they retreated in tight, orderly formation. Two American Air Corps sergeants whose unit had been overrun also joined me. Mortar fire landed sporadically along the way, and we eventually came upon an army transport truck that had been hit and burned. I paused to examine the scene, and one of the others started poking around in the charred ruins.

"Lieutenant, look!"

I looked over and discovered that the vehicle was full of C-rations, which were calorie-rich instant meals given to combat soldiers. Until then I did not think there was any such food left on Bataan. But I soon realized that those rations had been held in reserve for the front-line troops. It made sense; after all, our battalion had arranged a shipment before sending us into battle, but it never got to the front. If the intended recipients could not have the food, there was no use letting it go to waste, especially since it was fully cooked!

Betting that the same spot would not be hit by mortar fire twice within a few minutes and too hungry to care if it was, we stopped to eat our fill. The men and I used our bayonets to pick up the smoldering cans and enjoyed the Spam and corned beef. Then we collected as much food as we could carry and continued walking well into the night.

Around 1:00 A.M. we met a battalion that included several officers who came to the Philippines with me on board the *President Cleveland*. Theirs was a Filipino scout unit armed with machine guns and assigned to defend the road.

"Don't fire!" I yelled. "The Fifty-seventh Infantry is behind us, and they'll be entering your line!"

"What's going on?" one of the engineers asked.

"It is a rout," I said. "The Japs are advancing on all fronts. We're heading south. You should do the same."

More heavy fire erupted to our rear. The Japanese, who had actually *passed* us a few miles to the east, were now flanking us. Realizing things had fallen apart, the scout unit prepared to move out, too. After that, the other two men and I continued on toward headquarters.

The end was now upon us. Our forces were reeling and could not hold out any longer. Utter defeat was obvious. I looked at the men around me. Only stragglers were left. Like the rest of the Americans on Bataan, they had nothing more to give. That was when the unavoidable became clear in my mind, and I was finally able to resign myself to our downfall.

• • •

The two sergeants and I continued hiking toward headquarters. By this point, Japanese planes were bombing the highway, so we moved into the jungle and walked parallel to the road. It was a safer route but much more arduous. I had not slept in almost two days, and as we journeyed south all day, I became very weak.

After nightfall the planes ceased bombing the highway and the three of us went back onto the road. Under cover of darkness, the traffic fleeing south intensified tenfold. Soon the scene resembled the evacuation into Bataan on Christmas Day, as a protracted convoy of soldiers, trucks, and equipment jammed the lane as far as I could see. Unlike the evacuation at Christmas, however, this was a frenzied retreat by soundly beaten disorganized units. We were not falling back to regroup; we were running for our lives.

The appearance of so many vehicles was welcome relief to a trio of weary foot travelers, and my new friends and I jumped into the back of a passing truck and rode it most of the way to Mariveles. With an entire army using that one road, it was slow going. The trip took all night, and I used the break to catch some needed sleep.

Around midnight I awoke to a series of tremendous explosions high in the mountains ahead of us. "What was that?" I asked the others.

"Must be our boys in the rear detonating the ammunition dumps," someone said.

"That's smart," I remarked during a silence between blasts. "No sense letting the Japs have it." I closed my eyes and tried to go back to sleep, but the hullabaloo put me on edge, and I was unable to relax thereafter.

The entire region was raucous that night. A short time later, there was, of all things, an earthquake. I did not feel the quake, and to my knowledge it did no major damage, but there was a substantial aftershock within a couple of hours that got everyone's attention. Some of the men thought the oddly timed tremor was an act of God designed to impede the

Japanese. To me, it was just an odd natural coincidence, one that had no substantial effect on their advance.

We rode on through the night. Knowing I would need to be fresh the next day, I lay still and rested as much as possible.

• • •

Shortly after dawn the truck stopped at the camp of a Filipino division located about two or three miles northwest of Mariveles. The white flag was up and there was frantic activity as the men broke out their remaining food and issued whatever combat equipment they had left. The two sergeants and I looked for someone in charge to direct us to corps headquarters. Only one American officer was left there, and he was hastily burning official documents before the first Japanese soldiers arrived.

"Sir, I'm Lieutenant Gene Boyt with the 201st Engineers," I said, explaining that I was separated from my unit at the front and trying to reach headquarters. "What's the situation?"

"Corps has disbanded," the officer replied. "Everyone's heading into Mariveles to figure out what to do next."

When I asked about the white flag, the officer explained that after midnight General King had surrendered. It was the only humane way to avoid mass slaughter, and I admired him for taking that step. Faced with an impossible position, he wisely realized it was time to give up. The date was April 9, 1942. Seventy-seven years to the day after Confederate General Robert E. Lee surrendered his Army of Northern Virginia at Appomattox Courthouse to effectively end the American Civil War, the United States Army suffered a historic defeat of its own. More than seventy-five thousand men would soon be prisoners of war, and the heart of the Far East Command was at the mercy of Imperial Japan.

The officer went on to say that, although General King had

relinquished his command, he had not ordered everyone else to follow him. The men were free to do what they thought best, surrender or continue holding out. The prospect of surrender did not appeal to me. I realized there was no way to win the battle, but I was still unwilling to turn myself over to the Japanese. Given a choice, I wanted to keep going.

I turned to my two companions. "We can give up now or keep going and take our chances. What do you want to do?"

The friends looked at one another, pondering the difficult decision. "I really don't want to surrender," one of them said. "Me neither," agreed the other. "What should we do, Lieutenant?"

It was a tough call. In my gut, I knew that an escape attempt was futile. We would be caught soon enough, but running would delay our capture, and I was determined to give General MacArthur's promised rescue as much time to materialize as I could.

"Well," I said, "let's collect extra food and supplies. We'll hide in the jungle until tonight, and then find a boat and row across the bay to Corregidor. It's only three miles away, and the boys there are still holding out."

That sounded okay to the two sergeants. "Yes, sir," they said.

The sergeants and I then went to a supply tent to gather some canned food saved throughout the siege. We also selected new pistols and better rifles from the weapons depot, along with plenty of ammunition. Money was a critical commodity even in war, and I suggested that we try to find some. But everyone was hoarding cash, and there was no money to be found anywhere in camp.

The sergeants and I put on new dress fatigues, and I got a new pair of boots, which turned out to be a tremendous mistake because they did not fit properly and gave me terrible blisters. I also picked up a couple of new pairs of socks and underwear, which, as an afterthought, I tucked under the front of my helmet. I stuffed a half-pint bottle of iodine into my helmet as well. I knew from my ROTC training that iodine could be used to purify water, and I assumed that finding potable water would be a problem from that point on. I had few personal items left, and the only other things I took were my wallet, a fountain pen given at my college graduation, my mess kit, a canteen, and a canteen cup.

Loaded with as much gear and food as we could carry, the three of us departed camp and walked up the trail. We headed toward the western coastal jungle in search of a hiding place in which to bide our time until that night, when we could make our perilous dash for Corregidor. We never reached the jungle, however, because the plan changed radically after we departed the Filipino camp. Before going more than a mile, we encountered a larger band of American soldiers ahead of us on the trail.

"Hey, Lieutenant," one of my cohorts said. "I know those guys!"

"Yeah," added the other sergeant. "They're buddies from our old unit."

The two sergeants ran ahead to speak to the men. A short time later, they returned with unpleasant looks on their faces.

"What's going on?" I asked.

"The others are going to surrender, sir," one of them began somewhat nervously. "We've decided to join them."

"I see."

I was not surprised. The pair had not seemed too enthusiastic about accompanying me into the wilds. They were more comfortable following trusted friends. To them, giving up now felt like the best thing to do. And maybe it was.

I wanted to go on. But I knew I would never make it alone. Even with the added provisions, I was extremely weak. Had I managed to elude the Japanese and find a boat, which was unlikely, I could not have handled it well enough to reach Corregidor safely. If I surrendered now, I could at least stop waiting for the inevitable moment of capture. As I debated the issue in my mind, I realized there was no other choice.

"You guys are right," I conceded. "It's the only sensible thing to do." I hesitated, sighing. "I might as well surrender, too."

We joined the band, and all of us walked back to camp, taking a small trail leading off to the north. At the end of the trail, near the beach, was a big pile of firearms. We pulled the bolts from our rifles and threw them into the ocean, so that the Japanese could never use the guns. Then we disabled our pistols and tossed the useless weapons, along with our ammunition, onto the pile. Afterward, we resumed walking southwest along the main highway toward Mariveles, trying to anticipate whatever lay ahead.

Pretty soon we heard yelling from up the road. Around the corner rolled a Japanese tank with armed infantrymen riding on its outside. These Japanese soldiers, the first I ever saw, looked menacing. Razor-sharp bayonets in hand, they stared down at me with cold, threatening eyes. A truckload of Japanese equipped with a loudspeaker followed behind the tank, and a robotic voice boomed instructions to us in English as the truck passed. "Attention! All American personnel are hereby ordered to report to the airfield at Mariveles. Repeat, proceed immediately to the runway at Mariveles and await further orders!"

The announcer reiterated his message over and over with exact cadence and timing, as if the words were a recording. When the Japanese vehicles passed us, the enlisted men and

I stopped in our tracks. Just down the road ahead of us, another group of Americans panicked and ran. The tank soldiers drew their machine guns and mowed them all down in cold blood. Unfazed, the drivers of the tank and truck drove on, repeating the surrender instructions to every prisoner who crossed their path.

Nobody in our group said a word about what we had just seen, as if not discussing the tragedy would make it go away. As much as my comrades and I wanted to bury our fallen countrymen, the Japanese would have killed us if we had stopped to do so. As we walked past, I refused to look at the mangled, bloody bodies.

I gained something important from witnessing that execution. The Japanese meant business, and further resistance was certain death. From that moment on, I concentrated on doing what I was told in order to survive. It was too bad those others did not realize that. Their ill-advised escape attempt cost them their lives. Watching them die senselessly was a terrible sight, but one I would see repeatedly in the days ahead.

• • •

Now that we had been instructed where to go, I wanted to get there fast. There was an old Ford station wagon parked close by. The car must have belonged to a civilian because it had no army markings. It was obviously abandoned, so several of us got in and, with one of the men I did not know doing the driving, we traveled the short distance to the airfield on the southern end of Mariveles. At the edge of the runway, we parked the car, disabled the engine, and walked out to give ourselves up.

There were thousands of other prisoners standing around, and it seemed that most of them were American service troops, such as the 803d engineers. That was logical, since most support personnel had been concentrated near Mariveles, at the back of the American-held zone, when the formal surrender occurred. A lot of the regular combat divisions, like the I Corps and most of the Filipino troops, capitulated farther north near the front lines or along the western edge of Bataan. It would take the Japanese longer to round up all of those men and bring them to Mariveles.

When the guards approached, I was gripped by fear and braced myself for the worst. Scared to death, I tried not to show it. The captors lined us up in long, single-file rows in the center of the runway. Immediately, they became very belligerent, barking angry orders in Japanese, which few of us could understand. But as they performed the crude sign gesture of emptying one's pockets, it was easy to comprehend that they wanted our valuables.

For about an hour, the soldiers strolled up and down the lines, frisking the prisoners. To the Japanese, this was a serious pursuit. They meant for us to stand perfectly still while being searched, and they took anything they wanted: watches, medals, rings, photographs, food, water, or whatever. Those guards were able scavengers. In short order, they collected just about everything of value. It was not a full body search, however, and lots of guys found creative ways to hide stuff on their persons. (Throughout my internment I ran into men who secretly kept all sorts of precious keepsakes.)

As the mass theft began, an obstinate prisoner near me protested the loss of a sentimental item. "Hey, you bastards! Give that back!" The Japanese response was swift and direct: they beat the man terribly, continuing the punishment long after he was immobilized on the ground. That violent act sent a powerful message to those of us in the vicinity, and nobody near me objected to the loss of his possessions after that, although some down the line still had lessons to learn. To either side of me, I heard guards beating other defiant Americans, both before and after taking what they wanted from them. The display of brute force surely broke their will to resist, as well.

The first sentry to reach me took my cherished graduation pen, my wallet, and all of my canned food. A nearsighted guard later came along and took my eyeglasses. He put them on, and then shook his head a couple of times to check the fit. A broad grin told me that they improved his vision, and the glasses were no longer mine. Little mistakes haunt you at such times, and I wondered if I should have tried to hide the glasses. Luckily, I needed them only for reading, something I would not be doing much of any time soon.

Those Japanese seized a decent bounty from me, but they missed the bottle of iodine. Both of the guards saw it when they searched me, but it must not have meant anything to them because they left it alone. Retaining that tiny glass decanter was a huge stroke of luck. Had the iodine struck a guard's fancy, I probably would not be telling this story.

By the time the Japanese finished looting us, it was about noon. Soon thereafter, they counted us off into rows of about one hundred prisoners apiece, with two guards in the front of each column and two in the rear. Then, without explanation, they led the groups of prisoners away from the airfield and up the road to the north. Mine was one of the last groups to depart that day. When it did, my leg of one of the most hideous forced marches in the history of war—the infamous Bataan Death March—began.

CHAPTER 6

MARCH OF DEATH

We marched out of Bataan in rows four abreast, moving northwest up the coastal highway. I was separated into a different column from the group I had surrendered with and saw no one I knew, only the gaunt, desperate faces of strangers. Lost in that mass of anonymous prisoners, I felt isolated and alone. I fought those feelings by fixing my gaze straight ahead over the endless horizon.

The road was heavily congested. Some American and Filipino vehicles were still headed to Mariveles, the last stragglers to surrender, but Japanese trucks and transports constituted most of the southbound traffic. Thousands of enemy troops, carrying full field packs, were also marching down from bases in the north. Having been well fed throughout the battle for the Philippines, they were in good condition and moved efficiently in tight formation. I had to hand it to those soldiers; they were wonderfully trained and impressive to watch.

It was an odd arrangement as the two massive opposing forces passed within inches of each other. The battle was over, and no shots were fired, but the Japanese guards still sought glory from the encounter. With seasoned combat troops watching, they sternly prodded the prisoners along as if we were living trophies awarded for their valor.

When Hirohito's men triumphantly entered our territory, I felt very indignant. The flag they carried depicted a red sun, the symbol of the Japanese Empire. That sun had now risen over much of the South Pacific. Everything on Luzon Island, including the runways my men had worked so hard to construct, was theirs for the taking. Filled with anger, I walked on bitterly.

. . .

It was not long until the advancing soldiers started beating us. Any Japanese who could reach an American hit him with a fist, elbow, or rifle butt. Their blows were strong; some broke jaws and bloodied noses. They were rewarded for these heartless acts with cheers of support from their comrades. I quickly figured out that the safest place to be was in one of the interior columns, out of their reach. I also worked my way to the rear of the pack. That was a good idea, since the Japanese assaulted the front rows vigorously but tended to tire out before the back rows were within range. Throughout the ordeal, I stayed as inconspicuous as possible. It was one instance when I thanked God for being short, because I could duck behind the taller prisoners.

By contrast, the Filipino draftees, the first to break under the strain of captivity, were far from indistinct. As the march began, they tried on bent knees to convince the Japanese that they were really civilians and should be released. The guards knew better, and their false claims were often silenced with the swipe of a sword or the thrust of a bayonet. As I watched the Filipinos grovel, I felt conflicting emotions. I recognized their fear and genuinely pitied them, but I worried that their emotional behavior was annoying the Japanese, making them more likely to harm the rest of us. In the end, I was powerless to change the situation, so I just kept quiet and tried to stay out of sight.

I saw the first dead GI about an hour into the march. It was a horrible sight, indicating just how cruel our captors could be. The unfortunate American had been killed in the middle of the highway. What made the image so unnerving was the way the Japanese treated his body afterward. It was lying prostrate, arms and legs outstretched like a gingerbread man's, and not more than an inch thick. Dozens of heavy trucks had crushed the corpse until it was flattened like a starched suit. As I walked away, several more enemy transports intentionally veered out of their paths to hit the remains. Each time one did, Japanese soldiers hollered with delight; to them, it was an amusing spectacle.

•   •   •

After leaving Mariveles, we followed the winding dusty road up a ridge overlooking Manila Bay. From that vantage point, I saw about twenty thousand American and Filipino soldiers to my front and rear, the first wave of POWs being moved out of Bataan. At that point, the pace of the march quickened as the impatient Japanese pushed us faster. When we reached the plateau, I was exhausted. Gazing out over Manila Bay, I saw Corregidor in the distance. Twenty thousand brave American and Filipino soldiers were still there fighting, and I mildly regretted not trying to make it to "The Rock" when I had a chance the day before. But it was not a burning remorse, for I realized that those courageous holdouts would ultimately face the same fate as the rest of us.

The Japanese were preparing to storm Corregidor with thousands of soldiers and tons of field ordnance. I gazed in amazement at the hundreds of artillery pieces lined hub-to-hub on that coastal road, all aimed out into the bay. The Japanese wanted to subdue the island quickly, for it housed enormous fourteen-inch, disappearing guns capable of destroying an entire fleet before it reached the harbor. By maintaining control of the well-armed fortress, the Americans still effectively controlled Manila Bay.

The Japanese attacked Corregidor later that day. As I walked near the shore, I heard the explosive thunder of enemy guns and witnessed the terrible pounding that Corregidor was taking. I could not see its cliffs because a huge dust cloud from all the shelling hid them from view, but I knew a graceful sentinel of freedom was being reduced to rubble.

The garrisons on Corregidor held their fire initially because they did not want to harm the POWs. Eventually, they had no choice and started shooting back. Luckily, I had been marched far away from shore and was safe by the time they engaged the enemy. The guys farther behind me were in grave danger of being hit by friendly fire, however, because the boys on Corregidor thoroughly pelted the Japanese artillery positioned along the coastal road.

At nightfall we finally stopped so the guards could rest. Ominously, after a full day's marching, we were given no food or water. The columns of exhausted prisoners were also kept standing by the road for several hours. At one point, following a shift change, the new guards let us sit for a while. Oh, did it feel good to sit down! But when the next guards took over, we were forced to stand again for the rest of the night.

As the events of our first day demonstrated, conditions on the march were very tough. So many factors worked against us. The hot tropical sun drained precious energy from the men. (A substantial number of casualities resulted from heat stroke.) Healthy soldiers marching steadily could have covered the seventy miles from Bataan to San Fernando fairly easily in about two days. In our emaciated condition, that was impossible. The caravan also moved very slowly, particularly during the first couple of days, because the guards kept stopping us to allow their southbound forces to pass. When halted, we were corralled so tightly together that we could not sit down to rest. Even when it was possible to sit, most guards would not let us. And if we did not obey them, we were dead—simple as that.

I learned quickly to do as I was told, but it was not easy. Because of the language barrier, I could not understand anything the Japanese said. Kicks and punches often emphasized their incomprehensible commands. It was all very nerve-wracking. Half the time I was afraid to do anything, fearing a mistake would get me killed.

· · ·

As time wore on and prisoners began straggling more and more, the guards' tempers worsened, and the beatings increased. We faced an unknown future, and many were overcome by despair, but they got no sympathy from the guards, who killed with cold impunity. I knew that I ranked far below even the lowest Japanese soldier. For an American accustomed to civilized treatment, that was hard to accept.

For the rest of the march, I stumbled along like a dazed

zombie. I was thoroughly exhausted, barely able to put one foot in front of the other. Yet with each mile that I survived, I grew tougher and vowed to carry on, dreaming of the time when the march would end. Above all, I fought to live; as bad as things were, I did not want to die.

I thought a lot about my mother, sister, and brother during those long hours and wondered if I would ever see them again. No matter how I tried, I could not remember the last time I had been with each of them. My mind was disengaging itself from my body; my thoughts were often incoherent and far away. Most of all, I felt scared and sad—very, very sad.

The guards became more savage with each mile. The terrifying thing was, you never knew what would set them off. I saw an American general punished severely just because of what was on his uniform. The emblem of the Imperial Army was a silver star, and the Japanese all wore one on their caps with great pride. When a young Japanese soldier spotted the general with stars on his collar, he became irate. He ran over and struck the general in the head and face, then ripped his shirt off, all because the American was deemed unworthy to wear anything resembling the sacred Japanese battle star.

The Japanese completely stripped us of our dignity on the march. They did not allow bathroom breaks, and we were not provided any sanitary facilities. Men tried to withhold their bodily functions until the column was stopped for a few minutes, when they could drop their trousers and keep the waste from accumulating on their flesh. But if a person needed to urinate or defecate while marching (and we all found ourselves in that circumstance at some point), he had to do it in his uniform as he walked. And there was no way to clean off afterward. That was an awful experience, and it contributed dramatically to the spread of disease among the prisoners.

Sadly, such merciless handling led some Americans to turn against their countrymen. In general, many enlisted personnel resented the privileges of rank. Under the circumstances, given the chance to buck discipline, they became real troublemakers. Others irrationally blamed their commanders for allowing them to be taken prisoner and were determined to make them pay. I will never forget seeing a rough-looking private berating an elderly man because he was having a tough time keeping up on the march.

"Why don't you leave the General alone?" someone asked.

"Oh, so you're a general?" the hooligan shouted. "Here's what I think of generals!" And he punched the old man in the face.

In that unbearable climate, it was impossible to hold our forces together, and chaos ensued. The ruffians dominated for a while, but wiser heads ultimately prevailed, as new, more rational leaders emerged. Unfortunately, the transformation did not happen immediately, because our officers' corps had its share of bad apples. Prior to the war, some unqualified people were given positions of authority. We had a name for these unfit officers—"eight balls"—and they caused many problems. Some chastised subordinates needlessly just because they outranked them, and even instructed them to hand over any food and water they were hiding. Dealing with brutal Japanese guards was bad enough. Having to contend with unreasonable fellow prisoners made the Death March even worse.

• • •

Early on day two, I began to see many corpses along the roadside. As the men collapsed, one by one, they were killed and kicked into the borrow pits, along with the mud and feces. Many Americans died beside that highway, but their bodies did not accumulate in large numbers because the Japanese forced live prisoners to dig shallow mass graves in which to bury them. This was done to keep the remains from rotting and stinking, not out of respect for the dead, for the guards had none.

Around midday, as I walked near the back of the column, a fellow in front of me went down from exhaustion. His friends tried to help him; they arduously picked him up and carried him along for a few paces. But they, too, were extremely fatigued, and it became impossible for them to haul his extra weight. When the man fell again, he effectively signed his death warrant. The others had no choice but to leave him behind. I, too, had to walk around him and keep going.

As I looked back, a Japanese soldier appeared, Johnny-on-the-spot, to yell at him to get up. The condemned prisoner appeared desperate to live; he got to his hands and knees and attempted to crawl back into formation. The guard obviously relished torturing the doomed American, for he stabbed the man repeatedly in the buttocks with his bayonet. Moments later, when the prisoner lay flat on his back, I turned away. A horrific, high-pitched scream told me that the guard had impaled him, and he was dead.

Of the many barbarous acts that I saw the Japanese commit against POWs, the most dehumanizing was to cast them into slavery. When columns of enemy infantry passed to the south, later on the second day, I noticed Americans being forced to carry packs and other heavy supplies. The looks of fear and shame on those poor men's faces broke my heart. How I wished there was something I could do for them. To maximize their humiliation, the Japanese tied ropes around the prisoners' necks and led them along in the hot sun like animals, mocking them every step of the way. If one of the slaves collapsed from fatigue, he was bayoneted where he fell, and another unfortunate victim was brought in to replace him. I doubt that even the strongest men survived the ordeal. It is likely that when they reached their destination and dropped the cumbersome loads, those Americans, who were no longer useful, were summarily executed.

. . .

As the days passed, the lack of water became a serious problem. A person can go a relatively long time without food. But in that tropical climate, your body deteriorates rapidly without water. The weather was punishingly hot, and we were forced to walk mile after arduous mile with no refreshment. If you have ever played a strenuous sport on a blistering summer day, you know how thirsty you get. Imagine that feeling multiplied tenfold, and you'll understand the crazed thirst the men on the Bataan Death March endured.

The only water we could reach was in the caraboa wallows, muddy pools along the borrow pits where the animals gathered to bathe. The water, laden with animal waste, was extremely filthy. No one in my group could safely drink that squalid liquid—except me. I had something most other POWs did not: a basic understanding of chemistry and a bottle of iodine. At a couple of critical junctures in the march, when the column had to move off the highway to let Japanese troops pass, I had the opportunity to put those important assets to use. I quickly filled my canteen cup with the dirty water. Then I untucked my shirttail, placed it over the mouth of my canteen, and strained the water in. I lost a portion of each cupful this way, but my shirt fabric kept any solid excrement out of the container. Next, I poured in a liberal dose of iodine, which purifies water. I shook the canteen vigorously, and let it sit for a while. When the iodine had worked its magic, I had enough potable water to sustain me through five hard days of marching.

Other prisoners were not so resourceful. In time, more of them became crazed for water and overcame their inhibition to drink from those polluted borrow pits. Most did not know it, but when they drank that untreated water they were committing suicide. Ingesting such slime was a sure way to contract dysentery, and like so many hazards on the Death March, dysentery was fatal.

Early that evening an American ahead of me was driven mad by his painful thirst. He jumped out of the column, screaming wildly and begging for water. I hated to watch, knowing how the scene would end. As the insane POW ran toward a Japanese sentry, the guards shot him. It was the only time during the march that I saw one of our boys killed with a bullet. At least he died instantly; I know I would rather have been shot than bayoneted.

· · ·

One of the strangest encounters I observed on the Death March happened on day three. We were stopped along the road while the guards completed a shift change. As one of the young Japanese walked away, he paused beside a very sick man on the verge of collapse a couple of rows ahead of me. Without making eye contact, the guard whispered, "I'm sorry." Then he walked away.

The words, uttered very softly, were barely audible. But what caught my attention was the *way* they were spoken. The young man in the Japanese army uniform said "I'm sorry" in clear English! I assumed I was hallucinating. Could I really have imagined an English-speaking guard? I thought about it for a moment and arrived at the only logical explanation for what I had heard. The young Japanese soldier must have spent considerable time in America. What, then, was he doing in the Imperial Army? I assumed that, much like me, he was a captive. Perhaps the unfortunate lad, who obviously did not hate Americans, was forced into military service before the war broke out. If so, he probably had no choice; if he had refused to fight, they would have executed him. I did not begrudge him, for he, too, seemed to be in a desperate predicament.

As unusual as that incident was, it was not an isolated one. Occasionally I met other kind guards who allowed prisoners to sit down when the column was stopped or to draw water from community wells in the various barrios. These surprising acts of compassion spared American lives. They also kept me from viewing every guard as evil. I suppose that realization was a major factor in my ability to keep from hating all Japanese after the war. It made me remember a valuable principle: judge individuals by their actions, not by their nationality. However, most of the Japanese soldiers I encountered in the Pacific showed no mercy and treated the prisoners horribly. My animosity toward them remains resolute and complete to this day.

•   •   •

After my third day on the march, the sentries pulled the column off the road and permitted us to lie down in one of the borrow pits. The ground was very dirty. But with my tired legs throbbing and my blistered feet burning, I was not going to miss a chance to rest—not even if it meant lying in a pool of smelly dung.

Around midnight the arid weather turned merciful; it

started raining, and rained hard the rest of the night. I awoke and filled my canteen with fresh clean water. A lot of the men around me got a drink for the first time in days. It was a cold downpour, but nobody complained. Thankful for the rain, I lay on my back, welcoming the cleansing shower, and slept well most of the night.

When I got up the next morning, the storm had passed. But it had rinsed most of the muck from the area, and a pure, fresh smell filled the air. The sunrise filled the sky with inspiring splashes of color. Surrounded by the gentle blessings of nature, I experienced a moment of spiritual renewal. Just as I began to believe there was hope for us all, a cruel twist of fate brought reality sharply back into focus. When I turned around I saw the gravely ill captain who had been lying beside me. During the night he had rolled into the bottom of the borrow pit. The storm had deposited six to eight inches of rain in that pit, and the man drowned because he was too weak to lift his head above the waterline. Another senseless death, I thought sadly. How many more until it ends?

• • •

It was now the fourth day of marching. Incredibly, the Japanese still had not fed my group of prisoners. Staggering along, I had become so accustomed to hunger pangs that I hardly noticed the ravenous aching in my belly. Ahead of me, a small shadowy figure darted out of the column, between the guards, and disappeared into the jungle. I rubbed my eyes and looked again. Nothing was there. Surely I had been seeing things. I was crazy from the heat; the elfish image must have been an aberration. But as I summoned the strength to walk a bit farther, I realized the mysterious shape was more of a guardian angel—of the Filipino variety.

The unknown civilian had secretly cut a few chunks of sugar cane and placed them strategically along the road. A few other lucky men and I grabbed them and got some much-needed nourishment. The evasive Samaritan was not working alone. Throughout the long march many Filipinos secretly threw sugar cane into the road for us to eat. They did so at great personal risk. If the Japanese had caught them helping us, even in that small way, they would have been captured and killed.

The kind Filipinos also did their best to supply us with water. Each day we were led through numerous small barrios, all of which had wells filled with clean, life-sustaining water. Most of the guards, who would replenish their canteens and taunt us by binging on the cool liquid in plain sight, seldom let us have a drink. When the columns were stopped by a well, hundreds of severely dehydrated men were made to stand just inches from it without being allowed to get a drink. The water remained just beyond their reach, a tantalizing but deadly lure. If prisoners broke for the well, the guards bayoneted them. This insidious "water torture" drove men insane. But the Filipinos found clever ways to ease our suffering. Sometimes when the guards were out of sight, daring natives left containers of fresh water in the road so the prisoners could get a drink. I will never forget those people for their selfless acts of kindness. There should be a monument to them because their simple, yet courageous deeds saved countless POWs.

• • •

By the fifth day of the march, my group of prisoners had gone approximately thirty miles up the coast. In the early afternoon we were stopped beside the highway to allow truckloads of southbound Japanese infantry to pass. Grateful for the break,

I bowed my head momentarily. When I did, a Japanese soldier in one of the approaching vehicles had some sick fun at my expense. When his truck went by, he swung a wooden club that struck me on the head with a tremendous blow. Knocked unconscious, I went down immediately. The blow might have killed me, but the extra socks and underwear that I had tucked under my helmet before leaving Mariveles softened its impact.

When I came to a few moments later, my skull felt like it had caved in. But the massive headache signaled good news: it told me I was still alive. I was in danger, however, as I gazed about groggily, struggling to get my bearings. I was down and unable to get up—a bad position to be in. Wary prisoners stepped around me and kept walking. The Japanese would not tolerate my "disobedience" long. I was as good as dead. Yet somehow my luck was working overtime. Earlier in the march I had buddied up with an old friend from Fort Belvoir, Virginia, a tall, redheaded fellow named Tom Griffin. Tom was an engineer from Texas A&M University. He, too, had come to the Philippines aboard the *President Cleveland*. Now, as I lay in the road, Tom picked me up.

"On your feet, soldier!" he ordered with phony pomp, trying to inject a bit of lightheartedness into a dark situation.

"I don't think I can make it, Tom," I said.

"You can do it; all you need is a little help. Now let's go before the Japs see you."

Tom was every bit as fatigued as I was. Nevertheless, he found the strength to pick me up, and he guided my steps as I staggered along the rest of the day. Offering that help must have been hard on him because I was in such poor condition.

At the end of the day, the guards commanded us to fall out at the side of the road. As soon as we stopped marching, I collapsed. But the Japanese had not given us permission to lie down, so Tom tried to stand me back up. This time, despite his efforts, he could not get me on my feet. I was just too weak to move. My brain felt as scrambled as eggs in a pan, and my stomach was extremely nauseous. The situation looked desperate. I think Tom expected me to be killed at any moment. But again, that did not happen. It was getting dark, and the Japanese sentries either did not see me or simply did not care to walk over and bayonet me. Instead, they let me lie where I was. That unpredictable twist of fate was another curious thing about the Death March; for all their savagery, the Japanese were occasionally indifferent. At Bataan a man's survival depended not only on his will to live but also on which guards were assigned to watch him at any given moment.

We soon saw the headlights of several trucks heading north. Throughout the march, I saw empty Japanese transports being driven to the rear to replenish supplies. As a goodwill effort, the drivers occasionally gave Filipino peasants rides to destinations along the route. The convoy stopped momentarily near Tom and me. Tom, seeing how disoriented I was, realized that I would not survive another day on the march. A true friend, he picked me up and called for a couple of Filipinos sitting in the back of one of those trucks to pull me in. By doing so, Tom took a big risk with both our lives. But it was my only chance for survival. Once more, Heaven smiled upon me, because those Filipinos hid me as we drove north for the next several hours. Given the opportunity to rest, I began to feel stronger.

The next morning, days ahead of the other abused, exhausted, and dehydrated prisoners, I arrived in San Fernando. There I got out of the truck and blended discreetly into a column of prisoners waiting near the rail depot. After five grueling days I was one of the fortunate survivors of the

Bataan Death March. I would not have made it without the help of Tom Griffin, whose brave compassion toward me made him a true hero. Sadly, I never got to thank the man who saved my life, for he did not survive the war. But I will never forget the great things he did for me.

CHAPTER 7

HELL AT O'DONNELL

At San Fernando we were herded into a converted churchyard that served as a holding facility for prisoners. A high fence topped with barbed wire surrounded the yard. Several hundred POWs were there, and it was hard to find a place to sit down. I was reluctant to sit, anyway, because the ground was covered with human excrement. The early arrivals had dug a single latrine in one corner. But with so many men suffering from dysentery, it quickly overflowed. The gravely ill had no control over their bowels and could not help defecating right where they lay. By the time I got to the holding area, the place was absolutely filthy. Flies, maggots, and dead bodies were everywhere, and the odor was overpowering.

The prisoners had also constructed a crude kitchen, and upon arrival each of us was given a baseball-sized portion of rice and a pinch of salt. The meal was our first since the surrender. Starving, I gobbled down the food. But my stomach was nauseated, and I vomited after only a few bites. Disgusted, I gave the leftover rice to a man standing next to me and did not try to eat any more that day. It was foolish generosity; I should have kept the rice for when I felt better. But I was not thinking clearly. Besides, the stranger was so glad to receive the extra rice that it seemed I had done the right thing.

• • •

Thankfully, we did not stay in that terrible place long. After about three hours, the Japanese led us down to the rail station, where a narrow-gauge freight train waited. They put all of us prisoners into wooden boxcars. About one hundred men were crammed into each car, which could comfortably hold about thirty. It was so crowded I could not relax; the press of bodies held me upright.

I must have been stuck in one of the last empty cars, because the train started moving soon after I was loaded. Yet I was among the first to go into that car, which meant I was relegated to the rear. The doors were normally closed before the trip began, but the door to our car was broken and would not shut. The guards tried repeatedly to close it but could not. This malfunction may have spared some lives since, once we were in motion, a cool stream of air flowed into the car.

But that rush of wind was initially blocked by the standing bodies on board. Soon after we departed, men began to faint. Dozens succumbed to heat stroke along the way. I was in an especially vulnerable position, stuck against the back wall of the car. Bright sunlight shone in through the separation in the boards and blinded me. Out of water and becoming dehydrated, I ceased to sweat; an elevated body heat started to burn my skin. Needing more air right away, I suddenly lashed out like a wild man. "You stupid sons of bitches!" I cursed at the prisoners closest to the door. "Sit down so the breeze can circulate to the rear of the car!"

A friend of mine from the 803d, a first sergeant named Cliff, recognized my voice. He maintained a keen sense of humor through it all, and I heard him yell, "Give 'em hell, Lieutenant! Give 'em hell!"

That well-timed remark broke the tension, and just about everybody enjoyed a needed laugh. Afterward, some of the men up front knelt under the legs of others. Then a refreshing breeze blew through the car, and I cooled down some. Even with the extra ventilation, men continued to collapse from the heat. Many prisoners still suffered from dysentery, and the car became an unbearable mess.

• • •

We traveled north some sixty-five miles, reaching the town of Capas at about 2:00 P.M. At that point, we prisoners were reformed into columns of one hundred men and marched north along a gravel road. Once again, I saw Filipinos dashing out to place sugar cane in our path. We snatched it up in plain sight, but this time the guards did not object. The nutrient-rich liquid sustained us, and my group moved at a steady pace, covering eight miles in approximately two and a half hours.

Passing through a large gate, we followed the road up a hill until coming to a flat area dotted with wooden barracks. It was obvious that we were in a former U.S. Army camp, although I did not know which one. However, some of the fellows recognized the place, and word came down the line that we were in Camp O'Donnell.

• • •

Camp O'Donnell was built before the war to house and train a division of Filipino draftees. I hoped our treatment would improve there, but it did not. The Japanese had turned O'Donnell into the worst hellhole in the Philippines, with conditions even poorer than on the Death March.

The guards stopped us in front of one of the main buildings. Word spread quickly through the ranks, "For God's sake, get rid of any Japanese money you have, or anything else with Japanese writing on it!"

I carried no such contraband. But I saw other prisoners digging about in their uniforms and discreetly putting pieces of paper beneath their boots, burying them in the dust. They were wise to do so, for the guards knew that an American could only obtain those items from the body of a dead Japanese soldier. If a prisoner had defiled the remains of an Imperial warrior, the enemy would see to it that he died a miserable death.

Moments later a detail of Japanese soldiers swaggered out of a building to our left. They placed a small wooden table in front of us. Next, out stepped a scar-faced, bowlegged officer, whom I guessed to be about fifty years old. His name was Captain Yoshio Tsuneyoshi. He was the camp commander; he was also the ugliest man I had ever seen.

To stand above the rest of us, Captain Tsuneyoshi climbed atop the table. He started speaking loudly in Japanese. An interpreter stood beside him, and after every couple of sentences he paused for the translation. The interpreter, who was also Japanese, spoke flawless English. He was cocky too, but his arrogance paled in comparison to Captain Tsuneyoshi's.

"Welcome to Camp O'Donnell," Tsuneyoshi said. "None of you are honorable soldiers. You are all cowards who deserve to die. Instead, your lives have been spared by the benevolence of the Emperor!"

I rolled my eyes at the "benevolence" comment. Other men shook their heads and sneered. But nobody was foolish enough to voice disagreement.

The speech went on for about twenty minutes, and it was so ridiculous it was amusing. In a fervid tone, the captain shouted hatred for "cowardly Americans." He bragged about Japanese territorial gains and assured us that we had only seen the first of many Imperial victories. This, we were told, was going to be a one-hundred-year war. Japan would never quit fighting. The Japanese would conquer and enslave the entire American race and then rule the world.

Captain Tsuneyoshi's closing words, which stuck with me, were no laughing matter. "You captives are our enemies and always will be. When given an order, you will comply with it immediately and without question. You will also salute all Japanese soldiers on sight. If you do not, you will be killed."

I found out later that Tsuneyoshi greeted every group of new arrivals with the same intimidating lecture. Tsuneyoshi was a man of his word. He treated us like archenemies and showed no compassion.

• • •

Shortly after Tsuneyoshi's talk, we prisoners were patted down to ensure that none of us had retained any weapons. Next, we marched to the barracks area, where I got my first look at my new home. Rows of several dozen billets were arranged around a central point to form a villagelike community within the camp. Most billets were simply constructed, consisting of four bamboo walls and a thatched roof. They had dirt floors and bays on each side that originally contained cogon-grass mats for sleeping pads. The Japanese had taken the mats for their own use, leaving the prisoners to sleep in the empty bays.

The buildings were small, normally holding only twenty-five men, but the Japanese housed *one hundred* prisoners in each of them. As we crowded in, privacy was nonexistent.

Wandering around the grounds, I ran into a handful of men from the 201st Engineering Battalion. They were the only other officers of the 201st to survive the March. I was glad to see them, and we buddied up right away. Those officers, along with a dozen or so others from the 202d Battalion, had moved into a barracks together, and I joined them there. Our building, which had formerly been used for storage, was about two hundred yards from the Japanese headquarters. It was smaller than the others and built a little differently. It had grass walls and a thatched roof, but no sleeping bays. On nights when it did not rain, we slept outside, where the air was fresh. Otherwise, we slept inside on the dirt floor.

By this time, I had lost about a quarter of my body mass and weighed approximately eighty pounds. All the prisoners at Camp O'Donnell were reduced to skin and bones. We looked like Holocaust survivors, with ribs and collarbones protruding visibly. When men finally died of starvation, their bodies were just withered skeletons.

Despite such conditions, we soon began receiving very modest but regular amounts of food. Cook shacks were set up throughout the camp, and each barracks was assigned to one. Meals were served three times a day. They consisted of one dipper each of boiled rice and soup. The rice was cooked into a watery goo resembling oatmeal, which was called *lugao*, the Filipino word for "gruel." And the soup was no richer; the first few weeks, it consisted merely of squash boiled in salt water.

At this point, men who had thrown away their mess kits were at a loss. But the prisoners demonstrated their adaptability once again. Some of them had helmets, which made good soup bowls. Others tried to catch the *lugao* with their shirttails, in their hands, or even on flat pieces of wood—anything that might hold it.

I kept my canteen and canteen cup, so I was in good shape. The broths tasted bad but were edible, though consuming them proved to be a challenge because I had to keep waving one hand above the canteen to shoo the flies away. This proved to be impossible because they were so thick. Those big blowflies buzzing about your face made trying to eat a dreadful experience.

Our inadequate diet was not enough to sustain everyone, especially the larger men. In the following weeks the death rate at Camp O'Donnell reached fifty prisoners a day. Hundreds more were immobilized, too weak even to lift their heads, much less care for themselves.

• • •

I did not think about dying at Camp O'Donnell. There were times when loneliness and despair kicked in and I wondered how I would make it through, but I was absolutely confident that the Allies would eventually win the war and liberate us. Having no doubts about the war's outcome, I never pictured myself as one of its casualties—even though men around me were dying all the time.

Formal religion played only a modest role in my maintaining a positive attitude. I prayed while at O'Donnell but did so privately. I typically communicated with God as I walked alone through the camp or at night, when it was quiet and still. The American ministers held Christian services within the prison every Sunday. The Japanese did not seem to care because they never disrupted them. I went to one such ceremony, and it was enough for me. Maybe I chose a poor minister, but I did not care for the sermon. It centered on pleading to the Almighty for help, asking Him to strike down our enemies and free us. I certainly understood the sentiment. However, I could not believe that God was paying close attention to our problems. I felt that if God had been, He would not have allowed us to fall into that hellish situation in the first place. That type of vengeful preaching may have helped other men, but it was not for me, and I did not attend another organized worship service until after the war.

• • •

As prisoners at O'Donnell, we were absolutely free within the camp area, which was secured by barbed wire fences and watchtowers. The Japanese hardly ventured inside the sprawling compound. They just put us all in there and left us alone. A person could move readily among the other prisoners, look for friends, or do whatever he wanted. Still, most of us did not have the energy to do much but lop around.

I cannot blame the guards for staying out, for it was a wretched place. With thousands of men suffering from dysentery, the latrines had overflowed severely. You could not step within a hundred feet of one because the ground was literally saturated with human waste. Clean water was so scarce that we could not take baths; I had not bathed since being captured and was filthy. Even worse, there was no toilet paper. First, we used grass. Then, when that was gone, we used sticks. Finally, we used handfuls of dirt. In the tropics those measures were very unpleasant.

Without any way to launder their clothes, most men stripped naked. Many GIs carried small tree branches to swat the flies away from their unwashed crotches. Forced to live in filth, I eventually got used to the terrible odor of excrement and decay, but I never got used to the maddening swarms of flies that it attracted.

At the same time, we became infested with lice. About all a man could do to get rid of them was to strip naked in the sunlight and search his clothes. You could kill the lice by squashing them between your thumbnails. But when the prisoners got too sick to do this, lice overran their bodies. I could easily identify the dying because they were completely covered with lice.

A large building, staffed by American medical personnel, was used for a makeshift hospital. But those personnel, too, were sick and emaciated. With no real medical supplies and not even enough water to clean the patients' bodies, they could do nothing to ease the mass suffering. When the sickest ones became too frail to go to the latrine, the hospital became just as contaminated as the rest of Camp O'Donnell.

There was a Zero Ward for terminal patients, and those taken there always died within a short time. The Zero Ward was located on the ground beneath the hospital structure, which was elevated on stilts. Waste matter often seeped down on those patients through cracks in the wooden floor, making their last moments on earth sheer torture. Each day droves of corpses were carried to the north side of the camp. Selected prisoners tried to dig graves, but lacking strength, they dug only very shallow plots. When the rains came, those bodies floated to the surface. Few of the remains were reburied; most were left to rot in the sun.

• • •

After a few weeks, the Japanese began to recruit details of men to work outside the camp. They especially needed experienced truck drivers. (Few Japanese could drive because automobiles were rare in Japan; their common means of transportation were trains, bicycles, and horse-drawn carriages.) The Japanese typically took between fifty and one hundred men. Lots of GIs volunteered to haul in loads of squash and rice to feed us; some even drove Japanese army trucks for a variety of official duties.

Those men were willing to do such work because it alleviated boredom and allowed them to get out of that diseased camp for a while. They also met Filipino civilians who secretly gave them canned goods, sugar, and cigarettes to smuggle back into O'Donnell.

Soon a thriving black market emerged. If a guy had anything of value to trade, he could suddenly obtain all sorts of things. One of my bunkmates, a mining engineer named Lieutenant Larry Rackmill, became quite a hustler. He buddied up with a Japanese soldier at headquarters, who sent him out one day on a work detail. That evening Rackmill came home with a sack full of food! Included in the bounty were several cans of sardines, some big cubes of brown sugar (which the Filipinos used for cooking), a couple of gallons of chopped coconut, a few cans of guava jelly, and lots of leaf tobacco. We were ecstatic!

Always a cool customer, Rackmill made us keep our heads about it. "Guys, let's decide how to make best use of all this."

"Why don't we dig right in?" one of the men asked.

"No," Rackmill said sternly. "If we do that, it'll all be gone tonight, and tomorrow we'll be starving again."

"I agree," said another. "We should ration the food in small amounts each day, preferably at the evening meal."

"Good thinking," said Rackmill. "That's the only way to make it last."

That night Lieutenant Rackmill opened a couple of cans of sardines. He mashed them into a paste, and each fellow in the blockhouse got one spoonful to go with his rice. It tasted delicious! For dessert, we each got a small chunk of sugar.

After dinner, Rackmill said, "I need whatever valuables you've got." He was going back on work detail in the morning and needed watches, rings, and anything else that he could use to bribe that guard into letting him bring in more food. We gladly handed over whatever he wanted, and for the rest of the evening our spirits were high. Around bedtime, however, someone asked where we were going to hide the food. Somebody had to watch it between meals and at night.

We talked it over for a few minutes. Finally, Rackmill spoke up. "I think it's best if we let Gene look after it." The others agreed.

I was overwhelmed; it was one of the proudest moments of my life, a high point of the war. Those starving men respected my character enough to entrust me to guard the food and not eat more than my share. Although I was determined to prove myself worthy of their trust, it was not easy. That first night, I slept with the sack under my head like a pillow. The aroma of the food was wonderful (I swear I could even smell the canned sardines), and I was very tempted to gorge myself. Yet, I would have died before betraying the others and did not touch a bite.

Things went on this way for a couple of weeks. Lieutenant Rackmill left on work detail every day and always managed to bring back at least a little extra food. As the keeper of our secret stash, I had to be leery of other hungry prisoners, who would have robbed me had they discovered what I was hiding.

Occasionally, I took my evening meal over to the barracks of Bob Silhavy, my old friend. Silhavy also made it through the Death March, and we were reunited at Camp O'Donnell. He was in bad shape, and I was happy to provide him with a

bit of added nourishment, as long as he agreed not to tell anyone where it came from.

One day in mid-June, Lieutenant Rackmill learned that the
Japanese were building a dam on the creek that ran just west
of camp. The dam would be equipped with a pump to deliver
fresh water to the Filipino end of the camp, and Rackmill
talked the Japanese into letting him work on the pump detail.
Since the job required four men, Rackmill picked two other
engineers and me. We all reported to the Japanese headquarters.

We were escorted down to the creek, where we worked for
several days alongside a Japanese engineering platoon of forty
enlisted men and one officer. We filled sandbags to dam the
current and impounded enough water to install a one-lung,
diesel-operated pump on the side of the bank. The primitive
contraption did the job, and soon the Filipino prisoners had
an additional source of water for their camp.

The three other engineers and I lived in a little hut near the
construction site, about two hundred yards *outside* the prison
gates. For this to happen, the Japanese subjected us to what
they called the "Rule of Ten." If one of us escaped while working outside the camp, the guards would kill ten other American prisoners still inside. Thus, if the four of us had
successfully fled into the jungle, a total of forty other men
would have been executed as a result. The Rule of Ten was a
barbaric but effective means of control. My partners and I
never discussed escaping. We could not have done it knowing the consequences it would have for so many innocent men
trapped inside Camp O'Donnell, and there was no reason to
run. We needed to regain our strength, and all things considered, the four of us had it better than most POWs. Our hut
had electricity, and we were able to live outside the dirty,

smelly compound. The Japanese even allowed us to get regular meals from their enlisted men's mess.

Every afternoon we went there to fill our buckets with rice, fish, and hearty soup. The bad part was encountering the Japanese soldiers who resented us. We had to stand behind them in the mess line, and any guard who wanted to take out his spite would harass or slap us. This was a terrible experience that really tested my self-control. I felt dehumanized and ashamed at not being able to fight back. But to eat well, we learned to grit our teeth and endure the abuse.

• • •

In the middle of our second night outside camp, small rocks falling on the hut's roof awakened us. The four of us went out to investigate. There in the darkness were several Filipino civilians.

"Hey, Joe!" they said. All Americans were "Joe" to the Filipinos. "Shhhh!!" We quieted them, leery of attracting the attention of the guards. The Filipinos wanted to know what they could do to help us.

"You can bring us food," said Lieutenant Rackmill.

"Sure, Joe. What would you like?" Never shy, Rackmill rattled off quite a menu, asking for fresh vegetables, meat, sardines, salt, coffee, and cigarettes.

The next night the Filipinos returned with our smorgasbord in tow. Rackmill paid them with money he made selling black-market merchandise to other prisoners, and our new friends left. The four of us were in seventh heaven. With so much extra food, my stomach actually felt satisfied for a change.

Those Filipinos came to our hut almost every night, and we established a regular trading relationship. We now had enough extra food to sell some of it on the inside. One of us made false bottoms in the three-gallon buckets we used to haul well water. Following a changing of the guards, one of us went inside the camp to refill our buckets. But first we put food in the false bottoms, which we then traded for money or valuables. These items, in turn, could be used to pay our Filipino suppliers or kept as profit.

The American commanders at O'Donnell set a policy making it acceptable to earn a 100 percent profit on anything smuggled into the camp. Most prisoners, especially the truck drivers, demanded much more for their contraband, but my group honored the official policy and still made off like bandits.

By this time, my partners and I were eating so well that we no longer needed to take our meals at the Japanese mess. Nevertheless, we continued trekking up there three times a day for rice, fish, and the occasional beating. If we had suddenly stopped accepting their food, it would have looked suspicious, and our smuggling operation might have been exposed.

• • •

In late June 1942 the Japanese moved most of the American prisoners at O'Donnell to Camp Cabanatuan, a larger prison located in central Luzon where the defenders of Corregidor were taken after their surrender on May 6, 1942. By then, more than fifteen hundred Americans had died at O'Donnell, and many more were critically ill.

After the American prisoners were transferred, the Japanese converted O'Donnell to a Filipino hospital. Only certain Americans were to remain. Among them were the gravely sick and dying, some doctors, a few truck drivers, and my friends and I who maintained the water pump.

In an attempt to gain the loyalty of local peasants, the Japanese brought in doctors from an American field hospital at Bataan and ordered them to treat the sick and injured at O'Donnell. The American physicians had little medicine left, but they did have supplies such as clean linens, cots, and surgical, laboratory, and other equipment. They were able to heal many Filipinos, whom the guards subsequently released from prison.

Interestingly, the plan backfired. Those Filipinos were not dumb; they understood who had really helped them. Rather than thank the Japanese, they remained grateful to the Americans and were more determined than ever to resist the emperor's troops.

．　．　．

Not long after most of the other Americans left, Lieutenant Rackmill got sick. He went to the hospital, where I assumed he bribed the doctors to take extra good care of him. I did not think much about his illness and went on with my work. However, I was shocked a few days later when word came that Rackmill had died. The lieutenant was stricken with amebic dysentery and passed away very suddenly. The condition, which is rare in the United States, can be treated easily with antibiotics. Left unchecked, however, it perforates a person's intestines, and the victim perishes quickly. The news was stunning because Rackmill had been unusually well fed and in good shape. Now he was another victim of the deplorable conditions at Camp O'Donnell. It seemed those of us on the outside were vulnerable, too.

About a month later my worst nightmare came true when I, too, got sick. I started passing a painful, bloody mucus and knew that I had contracted some form of dysentery. Reluctantly, I visited the hospital. A corpsman examined a stool sample with a microscope and then said the words that sent me into a panic: "Lieutenant Boyt, I'm afraid you've got amebic dysentery."

I felt hopeless. Rackmill had contracted the same thing and was gone within two weeks. Now it appeared I would soon be the next to die.

"What can I do?" I asked in desperation.

"Well," said the corpsman, "the treatment of choice is the drug emetine."

"Do you have any?"

"No."

"Then what else can I do?"

He dithered for a moment. "Nothing, really."

I left the hospital believing I faced certain death, but I kept a clear head. Having survived the Death March, I was not going to give up without a fight. After all, I had a small fortune in contraband and a pipeline to the outside world. Now I would use those assets for all they were worth.

I went back to the hut and spent the rest of the day formulating a plan. That night when the Filipino civilians came, I told them I had a very important request. I gave them a note that read, "Emetine needed to treat amebic dysentery," and I instructed them to take it to the Filipino Red Cross. To ensure their compliance, I handed them one hundred dollars, a sizable sum of money in 1942.

The Filipinos took the note and the money and disappeared. For the next two nights, as I continued to get sicker, I heard nothing from them and wondered if I had been taken. Then, on the third night, rocks fell on the roof and I rushed outside. One of the Filipinos handed me seven vials of the lifesaving drug.

The next morning I gave the hospital corpsman one of those emetine vials, and he injected it into my hip.

"Come back tomorrow," he said, "and I'll give you another treatment."

I did that for six consecutive days. Each time the corpsman took a stool sample, it came back positive, meaning I was still infected with the deadly amebic dysentery. On the seventh day I took the last injection. This time, my stool sample came back negative.

I was relieved beyond words. "Looks like I'm cured!"

"Not necessarily," the corpsman replied stoically. "Amebic dysentery is difficult to kill, and it could reappear. To be safe, you should continue taking smaller doses of emetine for about three months."

"That's impossible," I protested. "I don't have any more of the drug."

The corpsman looked disappointed. "In that case, come back tomorrow and we'll check your stool again."

"I won't come back," I said. "There's no point. If the next sample is positive, I'd rather not know."

I did not return to the hospital, and I never had any more trouble with amebic dysentery. Apparently, those shots were more powerful than most. Or perhaps the extra weight I had gained made my body more resistant. Or I was just damned lucky.

• • •

The three of us continued to operate the water pump at Camp O'Donnell until that fall. On October 12, 1942, we were told to gather our things; we were leaving. The Japanese then trucked the remaining one hundred or so Americans down to Capas. There, we were loaded into boxcars and taken by rail to Camp Cabanatuan.

CHAPTER 8

ON TO JAPAN

Camp Cabanatuan was superior to Camp O'Donnell in many ways. Cabanatuan was well organized and relatively clean, with plenty of potable water—the most precious commodity in a tropical prison. The food at Cabanatuan was a bit cleaner and slightly more plentiful but still amounted to a starvation diet. Three times a day we were given boiled rice and watery soup. Those meals did not taste very good, but at least there were enough eating utensils for everyone to have a plate and spoon. There were also adequate latrines and a hospital that, compared to the one at O'Donnell, looked like the Mayo Clinic. Prisoners could even take baths once every three weeks or so, although I was not there long enough to enjoy that perk.

Yet the camp had a dark side that made it a depressing place. Many Americans died there, most from fatal illnesses they had contracted at O'Donnell. And I saw other prisoners summarily executed following failed escape attempts.

Cabanatuan's bamboo barracks were divided by rank. I was assigned to the one for first lieutenants and did not know anybody there. I soon befriended the man who bunked next to me, however, a Lieutenant Clarence Madden from Texas.

I was not at Cabanatuan long enough to get into the routine of its daily life. After two weeks the guards issued orders for fifteen hundred men to be sent to Japan. Both Madden and I were on the list. The news did not really upset me; at that point, I cared little about what happened. Whatever would be would be.

The day we departed all fifteen hundred of us marched out of camp together and headed back to the railroad station, this time bound for the shipyards at Manila Bay. As I left through the main gate, I saw an example of the guards' gruesome flair for decorating, which became my most memorable image of Cabanatuan: two severed human heads, one stuck atop each gatepost.

• • •

When we arrived in Manila, the Japanese marched us right through the streets of the sprawling capital city. Their intent was to demoralize the locals by showing them how pitifully weak and dirty the American soldiers were. The Filipinos were not pro-Japanese, and they lined the streets by the thousands. Almost to a person, they cheered and flashed a V (for "victory") with their fingers as we passed by. Such unwavering support in the face of Imperial persecution was tremendous for our morale.

When we reached Pier 7, a long wooden wharf extending out into Manila Bay, the small contingent of guards simply let us run free. The pier was well lit, preventing anyone from jumping into the water and swimming ashore. The Rule of Ten was still in effect, and that controlled everyone's urge to break away.

We had to wait all day on that huge pier, so out of boredom, Clarence Madden and I went exploring. We soon found a shower room, and I stripped to clean up. When I pulled down my pants, I felt a sharp pain as skin came off with them. My clothes had stuck to my body due to dysentery and filth, and I saw that my crotch was an open sore. I soaked and soaked under the cold water, grateful for my first opportunity to bathe in weeks. I also washed my dung-saturated clothes. Boy, was that a treat!

While I was in the shower, Madden investigated the other side of the pier. "Gene," Clarence hollered as I dried off. "You've got to see this!"

I could have kissed Madden, for what he had found amounted to a gold mine. Stacked before us was bale upon bale of pure leaf tobacco! Clarence had a pillowcase he used to carry his personal belongings, and we stuffed it full of tobacco. His makeshift pouch was now a treasure-trove worth more than money. In prisoner-of-war camps men placed a higher value on tobacco than on any other item–including food. I later saw starving men, within a week of death, trade their daily allotment of rice for a cigarette. Nicotine is not only terribly addictive, it also kills hunger pangs and stops your craving for food. As a result, there was a thriving black market in cigarettes, and the Japanese never really tried to stop it.*

Needless to say, we guarded that pillowcase closely.

* The Japanese gave us about three cigarettes a month, sometimes skipping a month. Most guys unrolled the cigarettes and used newspaper or whatever to make several cigarettes. Each one contained enough tobacco for only a few puffs.

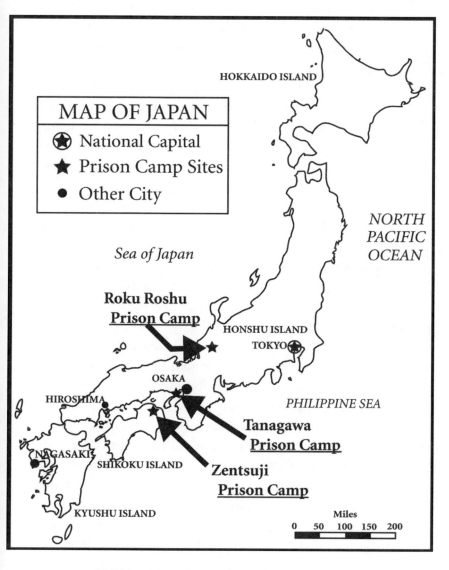

JAPAN AND SURROUNDING AREA

Clarence and I both smoked, and the tobacco provided us some needed satisfaction and a useful bartering tool for the next several weeks. In less than an hour, I had gotten a shower and found a load of tobacco. It was my best day in months.

We prisoners spent the night on Pier 7, sleeping on the bare wooden planks. The next day they loaded us onto a ship called the *Nagata Muru*.* The *Nagata Muru* was a five-thousand-ton freighter, small as such vessels go. Because the boat had previously been used to haul coal, its inner hull was blackened with a thick layer of soot. Converted into a prison ship, the *Nagata Muru* had three internal holds, one forward, one middle, and one aft. Five hundred men went into each. We were required to descend a ladder to the bottom of the appropriate hold. Madden's and mine happened to be aft.

The aft hold was not much bigger than the floor plan of a medium-sized house. It consisted of two levels, one being the actual steel-bottom hull and the other a wooden deck built about four feet off the floor along both sides of the ship. With five hundred men packed tightly into that confined area, many did not have room to sit down. Most prisoners, afraid of drowning should the boat sink, elected to stay in the center of the hold, close to the stairwell and directly under the open hatch. Madden and I realized that if the vessel went down, we would also, but we wanted to be as comfortable as possible and worked our way through the crowd to a far corner beneath the wooden platform. Few others wanted to stay there, so we had plenty of room to stretch out and lie down. Those in the center of the hold faced really uncomfortable conditions. At least a third of them had dysentery, and all were in very poor shape. Once we hit the open sea, the small boat

* All Japanese ship names ended in *Muru*, which means "ship" in Japanese.

started to move around quite a bit. A lot of prisoners turned seasick and vomited. The ship got so filthy that we gave it a more fitting name: the *Maggot Maru*.

Located in the middle of this mass of humanity was a large wooden tub that served as the latrine for all five hundred men. It did not take long for it to fill up, and its contents began slopping over the sides onto the floor. When this happened, the center of the hold became a terrible place to be. Each day the Japanese lowered ropes to haul the latrine tub up through the hatch and empty it into the ocean. On a moving ship, such "cargo" often splashed out and covered those below with a most unpleasant deluge. Each time that happened, Madden and I felt fortunate to be ensconced in our little nook, avoiding the downpour.

Three times a day during the voyage, the Japanese fed us by lowering containers of rice and soup down the hatchway. The food was prepared, as it had been at Camps O'Donnell and Cabanatuan, by American prisoners assigned to work in the galley. The on-ship diet was respectable. The soup was thick, and the rice was abundant. The food was divided equitably, provided a person was well enough to scramble to get his allotted share. Diminished physical vigor was not a problem for me. Since my sojourn outside Camp O'Donnell to care for the water pump, I had regained most of my strength.

In addition to the soup and rice, the crew lowered buckets of tea to us three times a day. There was plenty to go around, and I kept my canteen filled with it. To treat my crotch infection, I regularly took off my clothes and poured generous amounts of tea over that part of my body. The tannic acid worked as a fine antiseptic. By journey's end, I had gotten rid of that crud and my skin healed.

• • •

On November 17, 1942, we docked at Formosa, where we stayed four days until a dangerous storm passed out into the Pacific. During that time, the majority of POWs were kept in the three cramped holds below deck. I had developed cabin fever, and as soon as the swabbed-down *Maggot Maru* took to the open sea again and the guards allowed a few prisoners up on deck, I went topside. It had been some ten days since the original journey began. In that time, I had not had a bowel movement, and my screwed-up digestive system was getting more uncomfortable every day. Several privies were built on the ship's deck in such a way that they extended out over the water, allowing the waste to drop right into the ocean. One of them had a long line of prisoners waiting to use it, so I got in line.

To pass the time, I looked around and saw that two destroyers had appeared in a convoy of fifteen to twenty ships escorting us. I spent an anxious hour or two in line and was within six or eight men of having my chance at that *benjo* (toilet) when, suddenly, I heard gunfire, and there was frantic activity on the ship.

Our boat was not only carrying the fifteen hundred American prisoners, it was also hauling a company of Japanese soldiers who had strapped artillery pieces to the deck. Those soldiers immediately manned the guns and began firing at an unseen target. It was obvious they did not know how to fire from a moving ship, because some of the shells flew straight into the air, and others landed harmlessly in the water. They were lucky not to sink their own boats.

Evidently, we were under submarine torpedo attack, because the two Japanese destroyers sailed right past us at full speed, and I heard their depth charges explode as the rest of the convoy continued to fire. The Japanese began hustling prisoners below deck, but the Americans, sensing danger, were reluctant to go. The guards beat them with their rifles and the flats of their swords until they complied. As the line at the latrine dispersed, I hopped inside, where I tried in vain to take care of my ten-day-old problem. I stayed in there as long as I could, but when there were just a few men left on deck, I got out and rejoined the group.

I was one of the last prisoners to be beaten back into the aft hold. When we were all in, the Japanese boarded the hatchway shut. The sunlight and fresh air were cut off at that point. Worse yet, our only escape route was blocked. Now, if the *Maggot Maru* went to the bottom of the Pacific, we would all go down with it. I worked my way through the agitated crowd back to Madden's corner.

"What's going on up there?" he asked.

"Must be an Allied submarine attack," I replied.

"Well, I hope they hit this son of a bitch!"

My friend's fatalistic wish summarized most everyone's feelings. Life was horrible, and death an attractive alternative. It must not have been our time, however, for that episode passed, and we continued toward Japan without further incident.

After nineteen long days the *Maggot Maru* arrived at Kobe, Japan, on the island of Honshu. The date was Thursday, November 26, 1942. As I recall, it was Thanksgiving Day in the States. I was blessed to be alive; the dozens of men in our hold who perished along the way were not so fortunate. I do not know how many died ship-wide, but I later learned that one of the casualties was Tom Griffin, the kind Texan who saved me on the Death March.

Along with the deceased, 150 very weak men were carried off the ship and left on the docks at Kobe. The Japanese refused to care for them, so they must have passed away shortly thereafter. They were the first, but certainly not the last, of my group to die on Japanese soil.

• • •

Winter weather arrived ahead of the American prisoners from Bataan. We stepped off the *Maggot Muru* into a cold, wet snowfall. While living in the heat of the Philippines, many men had cut off their pant legs and shirt sleeves. Now, back in the Northern Hemisphere in late autumn, they were freezing. Luckily, I left my clothes intact. While I sweated more in the tropics, I stayed much warmer now.

From our port of arrival, all POWs were put on a commercial passenger train (there were no civilians aboard) bound for the city of Osaka, several hours away. The high-speed Japanese railway system was far superior to any I had traveled in the United States. Throughout the trip, I sat comfortably and sneaked a few peeks through the closed window blinds. We switched trains about thirty miles outside Osaka, at which time we got our first Japanese meal. It was identical to the ones domestic travelers received as part of the regular service. I am not sure why the guards gave us such good food, except that they did not have anything else to feed us. Those dinners were a veritable feast, consisting of rice, fresh fish, and seaweed, all bundled up in small bamboo boxes. I savored every mouthwatering bite; for once that year, I ate like a human being.

After arriving at Osaka, the fifteen hundred prisoners were divided into three groups of five hundred each. The first two units were sent to a location unknown to me. Then my bunch was marched to the newly constructed prison camp just outside the town of Tanaguaw. Camp Tanaguaw had solid wooden walls on three sides and a wire fence on the other.

There were five plywood barracks with dirt floors and two-foot-high bays along the inside walls for us to sleep on. The roof supports had ladders, which men scaled to a second layer of bunks overhead. Each barracks housed one hundred men. The camp also included numerous auxiliary buildings for cooking, supply, and headquarters facilities.

About 150 of the 500 POWs held at Tanaguaw were officers. The Japanese were dismayed to learn that they had only about 350 enlisted captives. It was a significant discrepancy, since the empire's forces had ordered all enlisted POWs at Tanaguaw to build a dry dock on the Sea of Japan. The structure was to be used by the Japanese Navy for ship repairs. Its construction required Americans to work long, hard days excavating a huge hole adjacent to a rocky inlet about a mile from camp.

There was a sticking point, however. The Geneva Convention stated explicitly that captured officers could not be forced to work.* Our senior officers reminded the guards about the Geneva provisions and told them that no American officers would perform any type of labor for them. We were not lazy; our commanders simply refused to aid the Japanese war effort. Most of the other officers would have liked to work, because, at Tanaguaw, the Japanese offered the prisoners three separate food rations. The first was for workers, and it was by far the largest and most nutritious ration. The second was for non-workers like me, and it was considerably less. Finally, the most meager rations were given to the sick and dying.

---

* The Japanese had signed but not ratified the 1929 Geneva Convention regarding treatment of prisoners of war. They agreed to apply the conventions on a *mutatis mutandis* basis. That is, changes would be made if necessary. This casual approach to the Convention was one reason POWs were generally treated worse in Japan than they were in Germany.

The Japanese were not happy about having so many "useless" officers to care for. Yet, surprisingly, they did not take immediate action to punish us.

• • •

We officers were placed in #1 Barracks, which was very crowded. I soon discovered that Tanaguaw operated on a strict military routine. Reveille was blown every morning at 5:00 A.M., at which time a Japanese officer and his staff inspected the barracks. We had to count off in Japanese, which was a real problem early on because some men had trouble learning the language. It was hard enough for them to count to 10 in Japanese, much less to 150. Most of us picked up the words we needed to know easily enough. Usually, prior to reveille, the senior American officers lined us up, and each man counted off in English to figure out what his number would be. He could then learn that one number and, hopefully, get by without difficulty.

Nonetheless, problems arose. Inevitably, one of the sick men fainted and had to be carried away. That threw the count out of order, ruining our plan and giving the rest of us a devil of a time. Fellows tried to help each other figure out their new numbers, but it was impossible to do on the spot. Someone always got it wrong. The guards were sticklers and made us do the count repeatedly until we got it right. It took our group several weeks to learn to count off to 150 in Japanese.

One barracks was designated as the camp hospital, and it housed a maximum of one hundred patients. The senior commanders assigned a trio of officers, aided by corpsmen, to oversee operations there: a Captain Tommy Thomas from Alabama, a Lieutenant Hap Ferrell from Boston, and me. All three of us were engineers with no medical training. Two American physicians were among the prisoners at Tanaguaw, and why they were not assigned to the hospital I cannot imagine. One of the doctors, William Marsico, checked on the critically ill and tried to ease their suffering, but he had no medicine and the patients were starving, so his treatment options were practically nonexistent. The other American doctor was too ill to assist at the infirmary and did nothing to care for the sick.

Under the circumstances, there was little my partners and I could do for the dying except to comfort them and keep the area as clean as possible. To make certain that no one escaped, the guards required us to keep an accurate record of the hospital's occupants for the daily prisoner count. During the winter of 1942–43, 70 Americans died at Tanaguaw. That was about 8 percent of the camp's population. Of the fatalities, 23 were officers and 47 were enlisted men. The total number of prisoners remaining at Tanaguaw on August 1, 1943, the day I left, was only 341.

. . .

When I had been at Tanaguaw for approximately a month, the Japanese moved most of the American officers to another location. About thirty others and I were left behind. Our new commander was Major William Orr, the most outstanding officer I encountered in prison. He was a twenty-eight-year-old West Point engineer and fellow Missourian who possessed the maturity and confidence of a much more seasoned leader. A stiff-backed, highly competent military man, Orr exercised considerable control over the POWs of Camp Tanaguaw. While some resented him, things ran smoothly because of his authoritarian approach.

What I admired most about Major Orr, and what separated him from other American commanders, was his willingness to go to the Japanese headquarters and boldly demand better treatment of the men. Most of his conditions were never met, but at least he tried. Major Orr's bullishness would have gotten him killed in the Philippines, but the guards on the Japanese mainland tended to be more controlled, and they generally used restraint when dealing with Americans. There were incidents of physical abuse at Tanaguaw, but they were the exception, not the rule.

. . .

By the spring of 1943, when we had been out of the tropics for six months, dysentery was no longer our deadliest killer. Now beriberi, induced by a deficiency of vitamin B_1, posed the greatest danger. Beriberi occurred because our diet depended almost exclusively on polished rice, which contained no vitamin B_1. We suffered from two varieties of the disease: wet beriberi and dry beriberi. Which strain a man got depended on how his body responded to vitamin B_1 deprivation. Wet beriberi was very serious, because it caused the body to retain high levels of fluid. This, in turn, led to organ failure and death. The symptoms of dry beriberi included extreme emaciation and gradual degeneration of the nervous system, usually beginning in the body's lower extremities. The legs and feet hurt in a way similar to that awful tingling you feel when they "go to sleep." Only this was a constant, excruciating ache—"electric feet," as we called it. The pain from dry beriberi made walking difficult. Some men had to be carried to the latrine. In the winter months they often stuck their bare feet out the side of their blankets to numb them in the cold night air. That was a bad idea, for while it deadened the pain temporarily, many of those prisoners developed frostbite and gangrene, which inevitably led to death. One courageous fellow in my barracks took the opposite approach. He walked constantly every night, bravely fighting through the agony in an effort to keep blood circulating to his feet.

I was one of the lucky ones who came down with dry beriberi. It truly was a blessing in disguise. Although dry beriberi could also be fatal, it developed much more slowly. That allowed me time to undergo a simple but effective treatment suggested by Dr. Marsico—finding an accessible source of vitamin B_1. The most obvious solution would have been to supplement our diets with fresh fish, but the Japanese were not about to waste their staple meat on us. Instead, Dr. Marsico asked them to bring us the nutrient-rich dark husks that encase rice. Eventually, our captors brought in tubs of rice husks taken right off the floor of the processing plant. We then ground these scraps into a fine black powder and took them in daily, teaspoon-sized doses. The vitamin B_1 in the powder ultimately cured those of us with mild cases of beriberi. It also kept new outbreaks in check.

In the hands of a compassionate physician like Dr. Marsico, those inert doses of black powder became a wonder drug at Camp Tanaguaw. I also saw him use the healing power of the mind in extraordinary ways. As the doctor talked to each patient, he asked what ailed him.

"Doc, I'm burning up with fever, and my body aches," said one patient.

"I see," Dr. Marsico replied. "Take some of this at noon every day for the next week," he said, referring to the ground rice husks. "It'll fix you right up."

A couple of days later, the man was resting comfortably, eagerly anticipating his next "medication."

Another man injured himself on work detail. "Soldier, if you swallow a dose of this powder first thing in the morning, it will ease your pain."

Sure enough, after taking the placebo, that patient felt fine all day. You have to credit the good doctor. Lacking proper medical supplies, his only alternative was to convince patients that the "drugs" he had could cure their ailments. Sometimes, clever mercy is the healer's best tool.

Many of us were also afflicted with scurvy, which results from vitamin C deficiency. To treat the prisoners, the Japanese gave us each a tangerine once a month. Eating the acidic fruit was downright painful, because with scurvy, the inside of your mouth becomes raw and swollen, and your lips crack deeply. Desperate for vitamin C, we ate the entire tangerine: peel, seeds, and all. Amazingly, those small doses of ascorbic acid did the trick. Our scurvy was cured in a very short time, and new cases seldom occurred thereafter. That was fortunate because in acute stages of scurvy, the body becomes one big open sore, and death can result, although I do not remember anyone dying from scurvy at Tanaguaw.

But staying well was never easy in Japan. We had no potable water because the fields were fertilized with human excrement. Over the centuries, this practice had poisoned all fresh water sources. Instead, the Japanese drank hot tea, which, when boiled, made the water safe to drink. They provided all prisoners with a tea ration six times a day in big wooden buckets. The only water available at Tanaguaw was for washing, and it came from a single hydrant and trough. Most prisoners did not bathe during cold weather, however, for fear of getting sick.

• • •

Fewer POWs were dying by the spring of 1943, although many were still quite ill. Those who passed away after that time were mostly the ones who never recovered from the effects of poor treatment early in the war. As a general rule, if a prisoner survived those first eighteen months, his chances of getting through the war were good.

A duty that I performed repeatedly at Tanaguaw was organizing details of prisoners to cremate the dead. Fallen POWs were incinerated at two local crematories. The one we normally used was a makeshift facility adjacent to a sawmill at the edge of town. Upon a prisoner's death, the guards brought in a two-wheeled cart carrying a large rectangular box. A group of about five other men and I would place the body in the coffin nude (the clothing was reused), and then pull the cart by hand out of camp and into the street.

The local people treated us with contempt. Most turned away or stood mute as we passed them. At the sawmill we would stop to gather discarded slabs of tree bark before proceeding about a mile to the shrine area. An elderly attendant would then direct us to the spot where a shallow two-foot pit was dug. Over the pit lay a steel grate, resembling those used on a barbecue grill, only much bigger. We would take the slab lumber and placed it beneath the pit, then lay the body on the grate and carefully pile more lumber on top. We always said a brief Christian prayer over the deceased before lighting the fire that would engulf his corpse. The others and I left once the pyre was blazing. The caretaker would continue to feed the fire for several hours until the body was reduced to ashes, which were later boxed, tagged, and stored back at camp.

I also made trips to the permanent crematorium in Tanaguaw, which was more like a mortuary. The body slab of the carbide furnace was on rollers, and the furnace had a glass door. That meant we could see the remains consumed by flames. But it was depressing to watch the fire char a person, knowing that his loved ones would not get to pay the last respects he deserved. So, after uttering a prayer and rolling the body into the oven, we departed quickly as it started to burn down.

．　．　．

Throughout my later detainment at Tanaguaw, guards pressured the American officers to work. One day, the Japanese colonel in charge of all prisons in the Osaka region showed up. We were marshaled into formation, and, as was customary when a representative of the emperor addressed a group of POWs, a table was brought out for the colonel to stand on. By placing himself physically above us, we had to look up to him, and, by extension, to the emperor.

The colonel made a boisterous speech, interpreted poorly, that began in the same old way: "Japan is engaged in a tremendous struggle to drive the evil United States out of the Far East forever! Everyone in Japan, including women, children, and the elderly, is either a soldier or a worker. The same is true for prisoners."

But as the speech went on, the stakes rose to a new level: "Therefore, all American officers will now volunteer to work. If they don't, they will be placed in front of firing squads and shot!" His tone of voice sounded like he meant business. Next came the million-dollar question. "So, I'll ask once more. Will you American officers volunteer to work?"

My eyes widened when Major Orr gave his defiant response. "Hell, no." I could not tell if Orr was serious, but I admired his bravery and was standing with him all the way.

It was better to die than to contribute to the defense of Imperial Japan. This rebuff drove the Japanese into a frenzy. They fussed and fumed and stormed about the grounds. The interpreter got in Major Orr's face, yelling at the top of his lungs. The guards roughed us up pretty good, but they did not execute anyone.

After being dismissed, Major Orr gathered the American officers in one of the barracks for a private conference. Though we faced death, there was little dissention over his resolute stand against the Japanese commander.

"As long as I'm in charge," Orr said in no uncertain terms, "nobody will volunteer to work. If anyone does, and I live through this damned war, I'll see that man court-martialed if it's the last thing I do."

"Yes sir," the others said.

Major Orr continued with some words of reassurance. "Now, relax. I don't have a death wish. If the guards actually line us up and raise their rifles at us, then I'll agree to put you all to work. But I won't do it a second before then."

The major's daring bluff worked. For a week or so, the frustrated Japanese cursed and hit us more than usual, but they did not kill us. Before I knew it, things were back to normal and we officers still were not helping them fight the war.

• • •

At Tanaguaw, I saw some American officers lower themselves by begging Japanese soldiers for food and cigarettes, but I know of only one act of treason committed by an American. I will not reveal the name of the prisoner involved, but he was an older man and a naval noncom. His bunkmates grew suspicious of the doting manner in which he acted around the guards. One day, when the man was away, they examined his belongings and found a letter he had written complimenting the Japanese government on its Greater East Asia Co-Prosperity Sphere, their euphemistic name for the empire they had created. The letter showed that the American supported the Japanese and was writing to volunteer his services as an experienced sailor in their war effort.

A few days later, the man in question was brought to the hospital. He was still working as a POW (apparently, he had not yet delivered his request to join the enemy). He had somehow fallen from a twenty-foot-high catwalk across the dry dock. Jagged rocks lined the ground below. I suspect that a bunkmate who had read the secret correspondence pushed him. Luckily, he did not break any bones but suffered only deep bruises. The old noncom wore false teeth, which were shattered in the fall. So he had to go the rest of the war without being able to chew his food. Nothing was done to investigate the accident or to punish whoever was responsible. The old man never blamed anyone, probably out of fear. I tried not to judge him too harshly. Although I have no sympathy for traitors, I think the fellow simply broke under the strain of imprisonment. Sadly, he was willing to do anything to stop the abuse and get more food.

• • •

No matter how bad conditions at Tanaguaw got, there were still comedians in the crowd who took any opportunity to pull an outlandish stunt. Sometimes the rest of us got involved, too, with hilarious results. We prisoners were still infested with lice because we could not bathe or wash our clothes. The only way to get rid of lice was to strip and pick them out of the seams of our clothes.

Someone on our side got the bright idea that instead of squashing the lice, he would collect them in a matchbox or can. He did this, and then one day, when a Japanese soldier headed for the barracks, he climbed onto the second tier to wait for him. As the guard entered the building, someone yelled "*Keotski!*" ("Attention!"). Everyone then snapped to. As the enemy stalked through the room, he passed under the joker hovering above. Our man then sprinkled live lice onto his head. It was a source of great amusement to later see that Japanese soldier out in the yard with his uniform off, plucking lice from its seams. We repeated that practical joke many times. Evidently, the stiff bearing of the enemy made him oblivious to the onslaught until he felt the effects of it. For us, it felt good to strike back, however subtly.

On another occasion, a day when it was drizzling rain, the guards shouted for all prisoners to fall in outside. Those of us manning the hospital did not go but watched curiously from the doorway. Out waltzed the Japanese colonel in charge, accompanied by a short, bespectacled interpreter we called "Goathead." The colonel then explained that it was Emperor Hirohito's birthday, and in his honor, we would be rewarded with "many things." (What we actually got was a single tangerine and a few cigarettes each.)

"Goathead" announced that it was customary to pay homage to the emperor by facing east and bowing three times. As we rose after each bow, we were to clap three times and shout "*Bonsai!*" ("Long life!") at the top of our lungs. When the command to bow was then given, the men bowed, rose, clapped three times, and yelled "Bonsai!" But in protest, the boldest of us substituted the word "Bullshit!" with the same voice inflection. The others then took the cue, and on the second time up, everyone clapped and shouted "Bullshit!" in what I can only describe as unified delight. The third time up, the cry was even louder. The Japanese could not understand why the prisoners were so happy afterward. "Goathead" apparently did not understand the difference between what they had said and the word "Bonsai!" and the colonel was pleased, thinking the men were excited to praise Hirohito.

It is amazing how often our captors were the foils of our mischief. As the war intensified, and experienced soldiers were needed at the front, the sentries at Tanaguaw changed almost weekly. The new guards all wanted to learn English and liked to wander about camp engaging prisoners in conversation. This offered yet another devious way for us to have fun. It was soon commonplace for some raw Japanese recruit, who had been tricked by a crafty American, to approach me and say in a warm, friendly voice, "Hello? How are you? My name is Mister Son of a Bitch." When this happened, I tried not to laugh. I would act genuinely impressed by his grasp of the language and warmly give my name in reply. Minutes later, after teaching him a little more off-color English, I would send the fool on his way.

I admit these practical jokes were juvenile, but we needed a laugh, and our stunts were harmless. They never endangered anyone's life, yet they boosted morale immensely. By entertaining ourselves in any possible way, we kept our wits while serving time in one of the bleakest environments in Japan.

CHAPTER 9

ZENTSUJI: THE OFFICERS' PRISON

On August 1, 1943, the other remaining officers and I were transferred from Tanaguaw. A short time later, the camp was closed, and the rest of its POWs were sent to Manchuria.

The Japanese trucked us from Tanaguaw to the Osaka train station. There we joined a band of one hundred or so other American POWs who were awaiting transfer and boarded a train to the city of Moji. We were then ferried to a dock on Shikoku, the southernmost large island of the Japanese homeland. We next marched several miles to the town of Zentsuji, where we entered a compound consisting of a pair of large two-story barracks surrounded by several smaller buildings. An eight-foot-high wooden fence secured the area.

Many other POWs were already living at Zentsuji, which had been established to house Allied officers up to the rank of colonel. About half of the prisoners were Americans. The rest were Australians, Brits, Dutch, New Zealanders, and Canadians. Most of the foreign personnel had been captured when Singapore fell on February 15, 1942, or they had been rescued at sea after their ships were sunk during naval engagements early in the war.

I was assigned to the junior barracks. It held all officers below the rank of major or its equivalent—about 350 of us total. It also served as the quarters for a small detachment of enlisted marines, originally stationed in Guam, who were working as stevedores on the local docks. The building was split into a dozen partitioned rooms that accommodated about thirty men each. We slept on platforms raised a few inches off the floor. Every bunk included a bamboo mat with three thin white cotton sheets, a cylindrical pillow stuffed with rice husks, and a small overhead shelf for storing personal items. My closest roommates were Bob Silhavy and Lieutenant Jim Baldwin. I had been with Jim's older brother, Barry, when he died in the hospital at Tanaguaw in February 1943. Jim was grateful that I had cared for his sibling, and we became good friends.

The other barracks housed prisoners of the rank of major and colonel—about two hundred men in all—and served as the Japanese headquarters. The outlying buildings consisted of latrines; a cook shack; a brig; a barber shop; a bathhouse; a chicken coop and rabbit hutch, used to provide meat and eggs for the guards; and numerous storage sheds. Several Japanese officers were stationed at Zentsuji, which was commanded by a captain who did not concern himself with our well-being. I remember one of the Japanese officers well. He was an older man, although just a lieutenant. We called him "Sake Pete," since he spent most of his waking hours in a drunken stupor. The fellow must have had some political pull because, no matter how inappropriate his behavior, he never got into trouble with his superiors. "Sake Pete" was harmless and did not bother the prisoners. One of the interpreters stationed at Zentsuji was a very sophisticated Japanese baron who had been educated at Oxford. He treated us with dignity. I always assumed that the highly intelligent baron knew which side would win that war, and I suspected his sympathies were not really with the Japanese military.

The second-story windows of the barracks were high enough that we could look over the fence and see what was going on outside the prison. Prior to the war, Zentsuji had been an army training post, and occasionally we saw detachments of Japanese soldiers marshaling outside. Also located near the outer camp was a Buddhist shrine dedicated to fallen war heroes. Priests journeyed there at various times to perform spiritual rituals, which we watched curiously from afar. Their religious services, very different from those practiced in the Christian world, were a painful reminder of how far removed I was from my native culture. We were forced to acknowledge their beliefs. Anytime a prisoner on work detail passed that altar, he had to stop and bow before it in reverence.

Conditions at Zentsuji were the best I saw in any prison. When you consider how wretched other camps were, I was lucky to be sent there. I believe the Japanese at Zentsuji were exceptional in trying to follow most of the guidelines of the Geneva Convention, and the sentries took a fairly hands-off approach. The guards blew reveille each day before sunrise and again at dusk. If the weather was inclement, we formed indoors. Otherwise, they pretty much left us alone. No prisoners were executed while I was there. The barracks and latrines were relatively clean, and the Japanese provided us with running water at outdoor spigots for daily washing and shaving. All prisoners were permitted to take a full bath once a month. We could also get monthly haircuts from other prisoners who were trained as barbers. By staying cleaner, we avoided being infested with lice. We still had bedbugs, but that problem was fixed soon enough. When the bedbugs reached the guards' bunks, they brought in professional exterminators, who kept us out of the barracks all day while they debugged the whole place with the chemical DDT. That did the job, and we had no problem with bedbugs thereafter.

· · ·

The big drawback about life at Zentsuji was the lack of food. The Japanese commander followed the same ration policy that was in effect at Tanaguaw—laborers got the most food; non-laborers got considerably less, and the sick got practically nothing. We officers who still declined to work were ingesting only about one thousand calories a day, barely enough to keep us alive.

I was doing well to maintain my weight at approximately 85 pounds (I was small-framed and weighed 120 pounds before the war). I doubt whether any officer in camp weighed more than 140 pounds at that time, and some of them were normally very husky men.

At Zentsuji they fed us three times a day. At every meal, both barracks received two large buckets of rice and consommé, which were then divided into thirty equal portions, one for each room in the building. Everybody monitored the allocation procedure closely. No one wanted to be denied even a single kernel of rice.

Our room had two measuring cans, one standard-sized and one supplemental. For each prisoner, the server (a comrade who volunteered) filled the standard-sized can, which held one cup of packed rice, and emptied it onto his plate. After everyone had gotten an equal share, there was always some rice left over. So the supplemental can, holding about a half-cup, was packed with rice and distributed to each man until it ran out. The next person in line then marked his plate, and at the subsequent meal, the supplemental rice started with him. We distributed the soup in the same way. This was a fair system, and as it turned out, each man received extra food at about every other meal.

After eating, we went outside and washed our utensils. Then a bell rang, and it was time for tea. The Japanese provided us with green tea three times a day: in the morning, at midafternoon, and again in the evening. "Teatime" became a real social event. I looked forward to each opportunity to visit with my buddies and have hot tea. It was the nicest amenity Zentsuji had to offer.

There were ways to make the most of what food we had. Men sometimes bargained with each other to obtain extra portions on special occasions. For instance, a person could give half of his rice from one meal to another prisoner and say, "Pay me back with half of your rice on my birthday." If he did that with several guys, he would have a nice satisfying meal on his birthday, or anniversary, or whenever he wanted. The hard part was sacrificing half of the rice one day to get paid back later, because we craved every morsel of food we could get.

Facing constant starvation, it was difficult to think about anything except food. One of the men's preferred pastimes was writing out recipes of their favorite home-cooked meals. If they could not have those dishes, at least they could fantasize about them in complete detail. Swapping recipes became a campwide practice. I saw fellows with books full of handwritten recipe cards; they spent entire days copying the best ones dreamed up by other prisoners. Out of curiosity and boredom, I succumbed to this craze and eventually bargained for five or six choice recipes, including those for German Cheese-Coffee Cake and Pennsylvania Dutch Pig. I never tried any of them after returning home and have no idea if they were really as good as they sounded.

• • •

The American officers' steadfast refusal to work was an undesirable arrangement for both sides. The Japanese wanted additional laborers, and the prisoners needed more food. Ultimately, our commanders cobbled out a creative compromise with the enemy that seemed to satisfy both our concerns. Located near the camp were four or five acres of fertile unplowed land. There the American officers would plant a garden. Technically, our activity would be labeled "exercise" instead of work. That way, it could not be construed as aiding the enemy. In exchange, we would get half of the produce we grew.

The Americans accepted the deal and became eager farmers. Not only was this a golden opportunity to provide ourselves better nutrition, it gave us something constructive to do. We raised several types of vegetables, including squash, onions, sweet potatoes, and *daikons*, which are about ten inches long and resemble a radish crossed with a turnip.

But the guards cheated us. They gave us *half* of the crops, all right—the stems and vines—and kept all the vegetables for themselves. We made the best of the situation by cooking the greens in a soup. I pretended they resembled cooked spinach, but I was kidding myself. The stems of the sweet potatoes gave some nourishment, but they included a milky white juice that upset some men's stomachs. I had no problem digesting the stems, which were filling if not very appetizing, and ate all of them I could get.

We were angry about being double-crossed, but there were also ways to cheat the Japanese. When work details went into the countryside to pull grass to feed the rabbits, the men often harvested wild onions and other vegetables. In addition, a few rabbits "escaped" and found their way into the prisoners' cook shack.

We were always thinking of food. So we anticipated eagerly the emperor's birthday in 1944 because the Japanese promised to treat us by butchering a pig for the evening meal. When the guards finally brought the animal in, the excitement level soared. One of the POWs, a rancher from Texas, volunteered to be the butcher, and he was instructed not to waste any of the carcass.

The Texan prepared the meat skillfully, and it was cooked in the soup that night, but my wish for a pork feast did not materialize. A single pig could never feed seven hundred men. The soup was so thin that the only part of the pig I got was a slight, fatty film that floated at the top of my cup. I was frustrated but not surprised. It was just one more disappointment meted out by the Japanese.

• • •

A navy physician named Dr. Van Peenen established a hospital ward in the #2 Barracks. Van Peenen worked tirelessly, trying his best to help prisoners in need, and his efforts did not go unnoticed. He gained the respect of the Japanese commander—no mean feat—who even provided him with basic medical supplies.*

---

* An outstanding officer, Dr. Van Peenen received numerous awards from the Allied nations after the war. He eventually retired from the navy as an admiral.

At Zentsuji, I saw how Van Peenen's complete dedication to healing saved American lives. Not long after we arrived in camp, a major died a very sudden and painful death. Determined to pinpoint the cause, the doctor performed a crude autopsy. It turned out the man had a locked bowel. After further detective work, Dr. Van Peenen deduced that the major died after eating too much burnt rice.

Burnt rice was a rare treat at Zentsuji. The rice used to feed prisoners was prepared in big forty-pound steel pots that resembled giant woks. When cooked properly, the rice formed a burnt crust about one-half inch thick on the side of the kettle. When scrapped off, the burnt shavings usually filled three or four gallon-sized coffee cans. We wasted nothing that was edible, so one of the rooms in our barracks got the burnt rice at every meal.

Divided among thirty men per room, the blackened rice crust amounted to about one-half cup of extra food for each person every week to ten days. To us, the charred residue tasted like popcorn and was a special pleasure. To get a full belly, men traded for extra shares. The poor major had done that with numerous people, accumulating several cans of burnt rice. But he ate them too quickly and all at once. That caused gas to build up in his intestines, which in turn caused them to lock and kill him.

It was a good thing Dr. Van Peenen took the time to complete that autopsy because a few weeks later my friend Jim Baldwin also suffered severe abdominal discomfort late one night.

"Gene, my gut's killing me," he moaned. Jim was ashen and literally screaming with pain.

Recalling what had happened to the major, I asked, "Jim, did you eat any burnt rice today?"

"Yeah."

"How much?"

"A couple of cans full."

I immediately suspected what was wrong. Silhavy and I rushed him over to Dr. Van Peenen. Sure enough, Jim had a twisted bowel caused by the burnt rice. The doctor performed emergency surgery to clear it, and afterward Jim recovered surprisingly well. Within a few days, he was back to normal. After that, we recommended that no man eat more than one cup of burnt rice at a time.

• • •

As in any prison, things at Zentsuji boiled down to a tedious, boring routine, but there were a few diversions. A person could pal around with friends, gamble, or read. Zentsuji had a library that offered a wide selection of books printed in English that were brought to camp from the former U.S. Embassy building in Tokyo. The library was a blessing because reading was such a nice way to pass the long, lackluster days. Some officers started "Zentsuji U," teaching free classes in their specialties. These informal training programs could be highly effective. Numerous men learned to speak Russian, for example, after being tutored intensively by other prisoners who were fluent in the language, and that helped advance their careers after the war.

In what seemed a magnanimous gesture, the camp commander allowed us to put on variety programs once a month. These shows allowed prisoners to demonstrate their various talents. One singer in particular, an Italian-American marine, was a marvelous tenor. When he sang "Ave Maria" with heartfelt beauty, grown men found hope and cried. There were also a number of gifted comedians in our ranks. One Australian was exceptionally witty. In addition, we organized intellectual contests, with question-and-answer formats similar to modern TV game shows. One prisoner, Louis Besbeck, who had worked as an assistant director in Hollywood, helped produce the musical *Sonny Boy*. One day during tryouts, he approached me.

"Boyt, have you ever done any acting?" he asked.

"A little in high school."

"How'd you like to play the female lead in *Sonny Boy*?"

"Why me?"

"You fit the part. You're small in stature and youthful looking. Plus, you don't have hair on your chest."

"I don't know," I said. "It sounds too embarrassing."

"Just try it. I promise you'll have a good time. And the fellows will really enjoy the show."

I finally consented and was glad I did. The producer was so skilled he put me at ease on stage. We rehearsed for several weeks, and he showed me how to portray female mannerisms, body language, and speech patterns. The costume man somehow found colorful material to make my dress—and boy, did it show a lot of shoulder! My role called for me to dissuade Sonny Boy from boxing and save his hands for violin playing. We all had a great time and at final curtain received a standing ovation from GIs starved for entertainment.

• • •

Zentsuji was a relatively civilized prison, but, the guards dealt harshly with those who broke camp rules—as I learned the hard way on at least two occasions. The first occurred when I was out working in the vegetable garden. At the end of the day, everyone was ordered to fall in before heading back to the compound. I ran toward the formation as instructed, but when I got halfway there, I realized I had forgotten my shirt and ran back to the field for it. Because of my backtracking, I was the last one to fall in. For that, the guard in charge gave me a substantial beating in front of the other prisoners.

The second incident occurred when Bob Silhavy, Jim Baldwin, and I broke a cardinal rule of the barracks: no one was allowed to lie on his sleeping platform during the day; we could only sit on them after the evening count. It was the dead of winter and none of us felt well, so we decided to rest a bit that afternoon, a clear violation of policy. Men regularly disobeyed the pointless regulation, and it was usually safe to do so because other prisoners near the door could hear the guards coming and alert us in time to get up before they entered the barracks. But the lookouts missed their approach this time. Suddenly, as my buddies and I napped in broad daylight, a menacing guard aroused us. He screamed in Japanese, slapped each of us across the face, and ordered us to follow him to headquarters. I was incredibly scared and had no idea what was going to happen to us.

The angry commanding officer was waiting in his office, and he explained through an interpreter that we had violated one of the camp rules and would be punished. The guard then led us to the brig, the inside of which I had never seen. It was a fearfully stark place: a wooden building containing six cells, each of which had rusty iron bars on its door and a single window cut high in one of its side walls. The cells were absolutely bare, with no platforms or furnishings of any kind. A rectangular slot cut in a corner of the floor was our latrine.

Before placing the three of us in the brig, the guard took away our coats; all we had to wear were our trousers and lightweight shirts. Luckily, the days were sunny, but with no heat, the nights got very cold. The only way my buddies and I kept from freezing was to lie in the spoon position three abreast, hugging one another tightly. We switched spots on the hour, so that every third hour, a different one of us was in the middle, which was the warmest spot. Throughout the night, we calculated the guard's routine, so we knew precisely when he would pass by the cell door. We separated our bodies just beforehand, because he would not have allowed us to huddle that way.

As part of our sentence, the Japanese cut our food ration. But our roommates brought us our meals and, instead of reducing the portions, they each sacrificed part of their rice so that we could have a little extra. Three days later, the guards released us back to the barracks. I was glad to have survived my stint in the brig, and I never got caught lying on my bed during daylight hours again.

I saw numerous prisoners reprimanded excessively for other infractions. The guards sometimes made men climb into a large tree in the middle of camp and stay up there for days with no food, blankets, or latrine. Or the Japanese forced fellows to stand at attention in the center of the compound all day and night, in every type of weather, until they literally collapsed from exhaustion. Both punishments were unnecessary and evidently served only to satisfy the guards' twisted sense of correction.

• • •

After spending almost three years in the custody of the Japanese, the other prisoners and I had learned to speak their language fairly well. We did not reveal that fact, however, because doing so would have been extremely dangerous. Once the guards knew you could understand their instructions, you became a marked man. Besides, in wartime, it was good policy to play dumb and eavesdrop on enemy conversations. We might overhear valuable information we could later use against them.

Several POWs in our ranks spoke fluent Japanese. Most were army intelligence officers, but one was a diplomatic attaché who had been stationed at the embassy in Tokyo. We cleverly exploited their expertise to stay informed about the war's progress. Men on work details picked up discarded Japanese newspapers and sneaked them back into camp (as prisoners, we had no access to reporting from the outside world). These special agents then scanned the papers for accounts of the fighting. The propaganda rags were full of lies about alleged Imperial victories, particularly concerning large naval engagements in which the Japanese sank American ships at places like Guadalcanal and Iwo Jima. Detailed analysis of those accounts revealed the truth, however. The battles they described were occurring progressively closer to the Japanese home islands, which meant the United States was pushing deeper and deeper into the heart of the empire and winning the war. Such knowledge cheered me no end. Perhaps, I thought, this awful war will end before long.

• • •

In November 1943, word came that Red Cross care packages had arrived from the United States. The news created tremendous excitement throughout camp. The parcels were issued at Thanksgiving, when I had been in Japan exactly one year. Each POW got one. The care packages came in eleven-pound boxes and were stocked full of supplies we desperately needed—boots, overcoats, and, most importantly, food. The Red Cross had filled each pack with compact, calorie-rich items. These included a box of sugar cubes, a can of powdered milk, a can of Spam, a box of instant coffee, a small container of jelly, a Class D army field chocolate bar, a tin of butter, and a box of either raisins or prunes. The Red Cross also gave us some essentials of the time that probably would not be sent today: two packs of cigarettes and a pack of chewing gum.

Imagine how overjoyed these starving prisoners were to tear into their Thanksgiving offerings! Those packages were like manna from heaven. The only mistake the Red Cross made was including the prunes instead of raisins in half of the packs. The problem was that the prunes contained big seeds that could not be eaten. That small variation made an enormous difference in the relative value of the two types of packages. I held my breath to see if I got one with the raisins in it. I did, and nothing would be wasted. At Zentsuji, every ounce of nutrition was critical to survival.

As soon as we opened the boxes, men began trading the individual articles. These guys had become expert barterers in prison. It was fascinating to see how the market quickly priced things differently. For example, the best brand of cigarettes was Camels, which were packed more tightly and contained more tobacco. A person could trade twenty Camel cigarettes for twenty-two Old Golds, Chesterfields, or Lucky Strikes. It was supply-and-demand economics at its purest.

That same Yankee ingenuity led the men to combine ingredients in strange ways to make different items. They mixed butter, powdered milk, sugar, and jelly to make a cream that to them was delectable. Other fellows added chocolate to the mixture, then poured it over rice to create a pie! Bob Silhavy, fellow MSM graduate Robert Powell, and I even fermented some raisins to make wine. We toasted our alma mater and sang songs like "The Mining Engineer" and "St. Patrick Was an Engineer." While I would not want to drink that stuff now, it was ripe for a celebration back then.

But the Japanese were determined not to let us have our Red Cross donations and their squares too. They calculated the number of calories contained in those food packages and cut our daily rations accordingly. So our total caloric consumption for the next several days was no more than usual. The prisoners grumbled about this discouraging blow, but they made the trade-off willingly because the treat boxes were such a delight.

Most men ate only a little of the food at a time, trying to make it last as long as possible, up to two or three weeks in some cases. I would not touch the Class D chocolate bar until lights out in the evening, when I was in bed about to go to sleep. I would then cut off a small chunk, pop it in my mouth, and savor its wonderful taste. I could even feel my heart rate increase as the chocolate hit my system. It was a great sensation.

The officials at Zentsuji permitted us to receive ten or eleven such food donations while I was there. That was probably more than were delivered to any other POW camp in Japan. The Red Cross also brought in a phonograph and a bunch of LP records. One room got the record player each evening. Then the next night, it went to another room in one of the two barracks. We could play it for a couple of hours after dinner and before lights out. We enjoyed new songs we had never heard and many familiar favorites by the Andrews Sisters, Glenn Miller, and Vaughn Monroe. I always counted the days until it was our room's turn to have the phonograph again. Even when it was played in adjacent rooms, we packed in tightly to enjoy the sweet sound of music.

The Red Cross was really a fine humanitarian organization. It eventually delivered some mail from our loved ones back in the States. This was wonderful because, until then, our families did not know our whereabouts. Officially, all POWs were listed simply as "Missing in Action." Now our relatives could rejoice a bit—at least they knew we were alive.

Once the Red Cross even brought individual packages sent from home. Some men never received a package, but I got one from my mother. Mom was smart. She had contacted the Red Cross office in Tulsa, and they told her the appropriate physical dimensions of the box, as well as the best things to include in it. She did well. The CARE package she sent me was very similar in content to those delivered previously by the Red Cross. It included many packets of dried soup mix, which was fabulous; powdered milk; sugar; coffee; and dried fruit. My family pack was the best that anybody in Zentsuji got, and some fellows had really good ones.

But one unfortunate soul received the poorest gift of any prisoner in camp. He had been an all-American lineman at West Point, and his wife sent him a football! The rest of us got a real kick out that—no pun intended. This well-intentioned delivery showed how little many relatives understood about our dire condition. When I saw him at a subsequent POW reunion, we laughed about the episode, but there was nothing humorous about it then. You could not eat a damned football, and nobody had the energy to play sports.*

. . .

In late 1944 we saw conclusive evidence that the war had entered its final stage: hordes of huge, sleek bombers (Ameri-

---

* Incidentally, this man was one who became fluent in Russian while at Zentsuji and later worked as a Russian language expert in the Pentagon at the height of the Cold War. In the early 1970s, he was featured in a *Collier's* article about all–American football players who had reached prominence in other fields.

can B-29 Superfortresses) began filling the skies high above camp. Each time the monstrous aircraft appeared, the guards, who did not want us to know what was happening, ordered all prisoners into the barracks, shut the doors, and closed the windows. But there were not enough guards to monitor closely all the men in camp, so, defiantly, we would crack the windows and gaze at the mass of planes streaking overhead.

Ten or fifteen miles away, a high mountain dominated the flat landscape in the vicinity of Zentsuji. We figured out that the American pilots were using its summit as a rendezvous point, because the bombers always came in on several different lines, then linked up directly over this mountain before turning in unison and moving on to their assigned target. It seemed that the planes were zeroing in on the major cities on the island of Kyushu, although Zentsuji was too far away from those locations to hear the results of their attacks. Several times during early 1945, however, we saw groups of small navy planes flying very low over the countryside. This time, we could hear the impact of their bombing and strafing runs as they demolished oil tankers located a few miles away. In all those months of aerial attack, I never saw one Japanese plane engage the Americans. I assumed, correctly as it turned out, that most of the enemy's air force was already destroyed.

Throughout the spring of 1945, as the aerial onslaught intensified, it became clear that America was on the verge of toppling Japan's military. At the same time, the Japanese intensified security at Zentsuji. They brought in extra troops, who guarded us more closely on work details. In May the rumor spread that the prisoners were about to be moved to another location. On May 31 our senior officers advised us that we would indeed be transferred, but this time POWs would be separated by nationality instead of rank. That was a significant point, and it caused us to celebrate in our hearts. We knew that the only reason for segregating prisoners by country would be to make it easier to release them back to their own governments.

The next morning, June 1, 1945, a Japanese lieutenant, whom I did not recognize, told us through an interpreter to assemble in front of the barracks. We were to march out the gate and down to the train station. The lieutenant urged us to move quickly and to stay close together for our own protection. He feared that local citizens, bitter over the months of destructive heavy bombing, might seek revenge against us.

We did as ordered, practically walking on top of one another and constantly looking all around, expecting an angry mob to tear us limb from limb. But nobody tried to harm us, and after a short hike we made it safely to the train depot.

CHAPTER 10

VICTORY!

At the Zentsuji train station, approximately three hundred American POWs crowded into passenger railcars for a one-hour ride to Takamatsu. There we took a ferry across the inland sea to the island of Honshu. At Honshu we boarded another train and continued on in the darkness (it was now close to midnight) to the large rail terminal at the city of Okayama. When my group disembarked there to change cars, the Japanese lieutenant again admonished us to stay close together and not to do anything that might provoke civilian passengers. We prisoners all huddled in a circle on the floor, and the guards stood watch on the periphery. As we waited, other trains came through the station constantly. At one point, air-raid sirens blared, and the locomotives sped straight through the terminal without stopping. Apparently, long-range American bombers had not yet hit this area, but it was obvious that the population was accustomed to air raids because none of the people panicked when the sirens wailed. By mid-1945, air-raid warnings were a daily occurrence in the lives of most Japanese.

We prisoners slept that night on the concrete floor of the Okayama rail station. The next day we boarded a train and were fed more of those tasty boxed lunches. This train seemed to pass through several cities because we made numerous short stops along the way, although I could not be sure because the Japanese had closed the window blinds before we departed Okayama.

When we arrived at the city of Osaka, we got off the train. Standing on the passenger platform, I could at last see my surroundings, and I have never seen such complete destruction. After months of continual bombing by the Americans, Osaka had been wiped out. Nothing was left standing except for parts of a couple of multistory concrete buildings. The rest of the city was decimated. An occasional person walked along the remnants of a road, but there were no other signs of habitation. For as far as I could see in any direction, the territory was nothing but a vast wasteland of junk and rubble—it was a wonder the rail lines had not been cut. After four years, fate was serving harsh vengeance upon Japan; the once noble nation was being reduced to ashes.

• • •

From the ruins of Osaka, we traveled northeast on another train, finally reaching the town of Fukui, on the north-central coast of Honshu. From Fukui, we rode a trolley a short distance and then hiked into the mountain country. We walked six or eight miles up the side of one peak. This was our most difficult trek since the Death March.

A few hours later the group reached Roko Roshi, a prison camp consisting of a single barracks building surrounded by a crumbling wooden fence. Evidently, this isolated facility was used previously for training Japanese artillery personnel. After marching in, we stayed in formation while the Japanese commander had an interpreter read our standing orders. As always, he gave us a stern admonition against trying to escape. The captain also declared that rigid discipline would be maintained and that we would be punished severely for destroying any Imperial property. I saw right away that even-handed treatment was over. At Roku Roshu, we were back under the iron fist of the Japanese Army. All three hundred Americans were packed into that one barracks, which had dirt floors reminiscent of Camp O'Donnell in the Philippines. It was so crowded that each man had only about sixteen inches of sleeping space. The guards were brutes, and from day one the senseless beatings resumed in force.

We immediately went to work digging a vegetable garden just beyond the fence. Roko Roshi was located in a sparsely populated expanse of open country. The prison was adjacent to a small town of the same name, but the only part of it we could see was an elementary school located about two hundred yards from camp. A handful of children assembled there very early each morning. They began the day by performing rigorous calisthenics, and then a teacher marched them into the school to begin their lessons. This was typical of the military indoctrination of the citizenry, and it included absolute loyalty to the emperor and the state. It was chilling to see this warrior mentality planted in innocent minds at such an impressionable age. The rigid lifestyle seemed to affect those kids negatively. I never saw them laughing or playing the way American youngsters did.

Our food ration was soon cut in half, which caused the men's health to deteriorate. The long-term outlook was not good. This area of Japan received about fifteen feet of snowfall annually. With no heat and improper nutrition, I feared that most of our group would not survive the coming winter. Morale plummeted; but it was boosted a few nights later when we heard warning sirens followed by explosions in the distance. The city of Fukui was being leveled, and the night sky lit up in glowing amber as it burned.

. . .

It was obvious to me that the Japanese moved us to this remote location to hold us hostage once American ground troops landed, as I suspected they would soon. We POWs could then be used for bargaining leverage: if the United States did not withdraw its forces, Japan's military would eliminate us all as a final, extreme act of defiance. In fact, the Japanese newspapers revealed that furious debates were underway in the Diet, their national assembly, about the fate of the POWs. Many Japanese leaders wanted to kill us if the Americans did not stop the round-the-clock assault. Formal votes were taken, but no majority opinion emerged. Even so, I never felt safe. I realized there was a real chance that the POWs would be put to death rather than released. I knew the enemy was capable of mass murder, and the prospect worried me tremendously.

I got so frightened that Bob Silhavy and I made a pact. If the guards formed what appeared to be an execution squad, we would try to flee and save ourselves. We would locate a map and mark a route through the mountains to a port city, where we could hop a ship to safety. Other prisoners might die as a result, but by that point, they would all be doomed anyway. In reality, this was nothing more than a ridiculous pipe dream. It would have been impossible for us to escape successfully under those conditions. Try as we might, we remained completely at the mercy of the Japanese.

Silhavy and I were not the only ones considering a breakout at Roko Roshi. One morning in late July, we all fell in for reveille as always. On this occasion, the guards were not satisfied with the count and made us repeat it several times. We were finally dismissed, and the rumor spread quickly that two prisoners were missing. It turned out that a pair of army lieutenants had absconded the night before. Their buddies who stayed behind told us that the pair had reviewed maps of the area and, after saving up some extra rice, broke out with a plan to steal a plane and fly to freedom in China.

The prison was abuzz for several days as we waited to see what happened to these escapees. The camp commander reminded us that the punishment for escaping was death. I was concerned that he would execute ten others in their place. But, in this instance, the captain seemed concerned only with tracking down and punishing the actual escapees.

A couple of days later, we saw a squad of Japanese soldiers coming up the winding road toward camp. They were leading the two Americans by ropes around their necks. The two men were taken away by truck to an undisclosed location, and we did not see them again. The Japanese commander explained triumphantly that they were being taken to Osaka, where they would be tried and then hanged. (I heard later that U.S. soldiers liberated them before they could be put to death.)

As this was going on, the guards developed much shorter tempers. If you did not bow or salute properly, or stand at attention rigidly enough, they would slap you forcefully. During the second week of August 1945, the Japanese captain informed our senior officers that the Americans had used "inhuman weapons" in the conduct of the war. Something enormously powerful had wiped out the cities of Hiroshima and Nagasaki, killing hundreds of thousands of people. None of us prisoners could comprehend what he was talking about. We advanced various theories about what had happened, all of them limited to a prewar understanding of technology, such as massive attacks with cluster bombs, nerve gas, or fire bombings. We had no inkling of the destructive power that had been harnessed by America's leading physicists, and our location at Roko Roshi was too remote for us to see the results of the atomic blasts. At that time, we could not comprehend that warfare had been taken to such a horrendous new level. The guards at Roko Roshi must have known the extent of the atomic devastation, however, because they became even more vicious about punishing our missteps and indiscretions.

• • •

On August 14, 1945, a truck came for the camp commander. He left abruptly and was gone for several days. After his departure, a curious thing happened: the harsh discipline from the guards slacked almost completely. Reveille was not required anymore, and nothing happened to a prisoner who forgot to salute a guard. My friends and I could not believe what was happening. What were the Japanese up to?

On August 22, 1945, the camp commander returned. He immediately called the senior U.S. officers to headquarters for a meeting. The prisoners were now going crazy. We sensed something monumental was afoot and gathered outside the door, awaiting news of what transpired. A short time later, one of the Americans stuck his head out. He delivered the sweetest words imaginable, the simple announcement we had prayed for since being captured at Bataan almost four years earlier.

"Japan has surrendered. The war's over. We've won."

• • •

It took a few seconds for the announcement to sink in. When my mind finally processed the news, I was filled with joy. We were liberated! I had withstood every dose of hell the Japanese gave me. At last, I could go home. The others were also overwhelmed. Men laughed, cried, and embraced one another like brothers. Someone brought out an American flag that had been kept hidden for years. We ran it up the flag pole and saluted triumphantly. It was our happiest moment of the war, a time most prisoners remembered fondly for years to come. That first wave of celebrating went on for some time. Then, as the initial euphoria subsided, it was back to dealing with the situation at hand.

Now in a position of power, our senior commanders demanded that the enemy officers relinquish their side arms and their swords. The Japanese complied without hesitation. The Americans immediately went about tearing down the fence surrounding the barracks. We used the wood to build bonfires throughout the camp.

Next, the Japanese guards were instructed to provide us with food and a radio. Before the end of the day, they trucked in additional rice and crates of fresh grapes, a wonderful treat. The Japanese also brought a radio, which we tuned to Armed Forces Radio (AFR), broadcasting out of Okinawa. AFR was transmitting continual news and information, verifying that the war was over and instructing American POWs to identify their locations by painting "POW" in white letters on every rooftop.

"Where are we gonna get white paint here in the middle of nowhere?" someone asked.

"Never mind," said another. "White bed sheets should work just as well."

Several men stripped linens from their sleeping mats and used them to make an enormous "POW" sign on the barracks roof. By that time, army intelligence personnel knew the location of most prisoner-of-war camps, but since Roko Roshi was a newly converted facility high in the mountains, our forces were unaware it existed. The intelligence officers in camp told us to be patient; it might take several days for American planes to find us.

With Japan's surrender, the Imperial Army fell apart. The captain and some of the guards left camp right away. Others, presumably uncertain what to do next, stayed behind. We former POWs had our freedom, but none of us was familiar with the area, and we did not have any way out of the mountains. So we stayed at Roko Roshi, too, although men soon began to venture away from camp. Some of them even went into town and were invited into the homes of Japanese civilians.

• • •

A few days after the surrender, we saw American planes fly high over the camp. Everyone ran outside, jumped up and down and waved, trying to get the pilots' attention. But the aircraft were too far away for them to see us. More time passed, and still no one came for us. Then finally, one day, a single plane flew by high above. Again, everyone ran outside to signal our location. The pilots continued on until they were nearly out of sight. I thought they too had missed seeing us, but the plane came back, flying very low, and thundered directly over the barracks. Then it ascended, turned, and disappeared. The whole bunch of us cheered. We knew they had found us!

Within an hour of the fly-over, our senior officers heard on the radio that food would be dropped to us. Doctors warned that because our shrunken stomachs were used to such a bland diet, we could not tolerate much rich American food at first. To avoid making ourselves sick, we should gather all of the food and give it to the camp cooks, who would then prepare and serve it in small portions under medical supervision. Everyone agreed that was the sensible thing to do and promised to follow the doctors' instructions.

Then here came an armada of planes. The sky was filled with parachutes as they dropped provisions stored in fifty-gallon metal drums. Some containers consisted of two drums welded together, and others were full of canned goods. This made them so heavy that the chute lines broke. Those barrels came to earth with the full force of gravity, just like bombs. The drop target was the barracks right in the center of camp, and we had to scramble into the countryside to keep from getting hit. Ironically, we were fleeing to get away from the hail of supplies meant to save us. The scene was comical, but the danger was real. One of those metal drums went right through the barracks roof. Another glanced off the building and hit a Japanese soldier, breaking his arm.

When the supply drop ended, the landscape around Roko Roshi was littered with metal drums. As soon as it was safe to return to camp, the mad dash to break them open began. And what treasures they held: cigarettes, clothes, medicine— and food, lots and lots of food! Cases of Spam, canned beans and stew, and even beer were suddenly ours for the taking. Within a few minutes, each man had a fire going in front of his barrels, ready to *quan* a meal. (*Quan* was a term we picked up in the Philippines. Loosely translated, it meant "miscellaneous." To *quan* a meal was to combine various items in different ways to create unusual but filling dishes.) To hell with the agreement to collect the food and turn it over to the cooks. It was too tempting, so we started eating right away.

Naturally, men gorged themselves. And as warned, many of them got very sick. They vomited almost immediately but were undeterred and went back to eat more. Our bodies craved the calories to rebuild tissue, and everyone in camp ate and ate. Dozens of men woke up every night, built new fires, and started eating again. They had not seen this much food in ages and were going to enjoy every bit of it. I was the same way; anytime I could hold another bite, I took it. We were also drinking lots of beer, which was loaded with calories, and trading for new khaki uniforms in the correct size.

Roko Roshi was surrounded by prairie. There were no trees, and wood for cooking and signal fires was at a premium. When the wood from the fence was gone, men started dismantling the barracks building. They built a big bonfire in the middle of camp, which we sat around while drinking beer and celebrating our victory over Japan. I could not believe it. This former prison now resembled a college fraternity!

• • •

Some time later, our senior commander, Colonel Earnest B. Miller, sent Major Orr into town to try to contact the American forces to transport us out of the area. Major Orr was gone several days, and I became concerned for his safety. Then one afternoon, a large convoy rumbled toward us up the mountainside. It was a platoon of U.S. troops from the 1st Cavalry Division. As we watched in wonder, they jumped out of their trucks, machine guns at the ready, and established a perimeter around the camp, prepared to defend us. My friends and I laughed; all we had going was a beer bust. The only danger was getting sick off too much rich food and alcohol. That light moment was something of a watershed. It convinced me that I was safe and that it was time to relax and enjoy life again.

The Rangers, who were expecting a fierce battle to save us, were visibly relieved. They loosened up but quickly got things organized just the same. A young lieutenant was in charge of the Rangers, and he sat down with each of us to record our personal information. The unit included a couple of nurses, who gave us basic physicals. They were a fine sight. After three and a half years in Japan, I had forgotten how beautiful American women were.

By the time they catalogued our necessary information, it was too late to leave the area that day, so we all stayed there overnight. The Rangers were very interested to hear about our experiences in prison, and we were eager to share them. A bunch of us stayed up late into the night talking with our new friends.

Around noon the next day, everyone packed up and got into the trucks. We then rode down the mountain and into the city of Fukui, which had been destroyed shortly before the Japanese surrender. I saw right away that our former enemy had begun the task of political damage control. In a transparent attempt to show the world how well the empire cared for its American POWs, uniformed Red Cross volunteers, who offered us hot tea and sweet rolls, met us at the rail yard, the first such gesture we had seen while in Japan. I took my fill of their snacks but was not fooled by the phony display of compassion.

We had to wait several hours for our train to arrive, and during that time the fellows explored the area. When they returned, some of them were carrying Japanese battle swords.

"Where'd you get that," I asked one of the men, thinking a sword would make a fine souvenir.

"At the armory just down the road. It's full of stuff that's yours for the taking."

I walked to the armory and found the building filled with unused military equipment. I took a sword and scabbard and then returned to the rail station. As we continued to wait, the Ranger lieutenant in charge noticed the swords and got upset.

"I've got orders that there's to be absolutely no looting by American personnel."

"Come on, Lieutenant," we protested. "It's just a few swords."

"The Lieutenant's right," seconded Colonel Miller. "You men take those things back where you found them."

Others did as they were told, but I refused to give my sword back to the Japanese, so I broke it and threw it away. That night our group of former POWs took a train with spacious accommodations to Yokohama. There General Robert L. Eichelberger, commander of the U.S. Eighth Army, met us at the depot. The good general showed real appreciation for our sacrifice and welcomed us as ceremoniously as possible. His band played patriotic music, and a detachment of white hel-meted MPs extended their swords as we exited the train. Eichelberger even stood there and shook hands with each of us. I felt special that day and always had great respect for Gen-eral Eichelberger after that.

Some of the boys, apparently with less regard for author-ity, had hidden their swords and kept them.

"Oh, you got souvenirs," the general said when he saw those men at Yokohama. "Good for you. Hold on to them. They'll be worth a lot some day."

Upon hearing this, I felt sick knowing that I had been cheated. Few of the higher-ups cared whether we took swords; it would have been fine for me to keep mine. I later heard that one senior American officer kept an Imperial battle sword for himself. Apparently, the man justified his action by claiming it was a "gift."

• • •

From the train station, they trucked us down to one of the few intact docks remaining on the harbor. We entered an enormous USO building with lots of army personnel all around. The International Red Cross served a delicious pancake breakfast while everyone took turns showering before being issued new dress khakis.

Suddenly, a bunch of MPs came hustling in, followed closely by a slew of high-ranking officers and photographers. Then, before I had time to react, General MacArthur stepped through the door.

"Attention!" yelled one of his aides, and everyone obeyed.

"Have them stand at ease," MacArthur said. The order was given, and we relaxed.

I watched MacArthur closely as he walked down the line, his corncob pipe in hand. The photographers snapped picture after picture. This was a memorable photo opportunity, the general greeting a remnant of his defeated Philippine command. As MacArthur continued to inspect the troops, he happened to stop about ten feet from where I was standing, so I got a really good look at his haughty face. I waited to hear the speech he would surely make, thinking he must have plenty to say to us. But MacArthur only posed for a few more pictures and then walked out without ever saying a word to any of us. I could not believe his callousness. Here we were, those who suffered unimaginably to buy time for his escape from Bataan during the lowest moments of the war, and now he considered himself too important to speak to any of us.

As MacArthur departed, a person near me whispered under his breath, "You SOB." I felt the same way and quietly seconded the opinion. How could such a "great" leader be so thoughtless and ungrateful?

It was the last time I saw MacArthur in person. After that disappointing encounter, I wanted nothing more to do with him.

CHAPTER 11

THE GOOD LIFE

Hours later, I boarded the hospital ship USS *Goodhue* bound for Manila. The American military presence was now everywhere in Japan. Beautiful P-38 fighters, mass-produced during the war, flew low over the water. I had not seen many of them, and each time one streaked by I felt like cheering. As it departed Yokohama Harbor, the *Goodhue* passed an enormous Japanese battleship at anchor. Alongside the enemy vessel were two U.S. battleships. One of them was the *Missouri*, on which MacArthur formally accepted the Imperial surrender on September 2, 1945. The American ships, in a symbolic show of dominance, had their guns leveled directly at the Japanese ship. It was a very imposing sight that left no doubt which side was in control of the islands.

As we sailed out into the ocean, I stood on deck and peered back at Japan for the last time. I thought about how far I had come in the previous four years. The ups and downs I had experienced seemed unbelievable. In 1941 I was on the fast track to a promising army career, full of youthful enthusiasm, but the war intervened and took all that away. The physical agony I had endured paled in comparison to the emotional scars I bore after surviving some of the most brutal treatment imaginable. Now I felt aged beyond my twenty-eight years, and all I wanted was to get home and begin rebuilding my life.

My personal renewal got off to a good start. The two-week trip on board the USS *Goodhue* was pleasant and relaxing. The captain knew how starved we were, and he stacked the tables at each meal with every type of food in his galley. The captain later said he was amazed that, no matter how much food the stewards put before us, there were never any scraps when we finished. We ate everything in sight.

I spent the bulk of my time resting and eating. I also read a lot, particularly newspapers and magazines, trying to catch up on world events of the previous four years. So many significant things had happened during my captivity that it was hard to comprehend the changes. Among the milestones I missed were President Roosevelt's death, the fall of Nazi Germany and Adolf Hitler's suicide, and the development and use of the A-bomb.

• • •

The ship arrived in Manila Bay on September 30, 1945, and we were trucked a few miles south to a large tent city established near the Twenty-ninth Replacement Depot. The entire area had been cleared and readied for the influx of POWs arriving from Japan. They treated us well. The tents were large and clean. Six men were assigned to each one and slept there comfortably. The canteens were always open to us, and anything we wanted was free. The camp doctors determined that the best way to supply our bodies with needed Vitamin B, as well as to pack in calories, was with beer. So each former prisoner was given a ration of three beers per day. While recuperating and awaiting further orders, we listened to the music that played all day on loudspeakers positioned throughout the camp.

I went into Manila on several occasions. Once, on the steps of the headquarters building, I ran into Colonel Wendell Fertig, my senior officer at Clark Field and the former leader of guerilla forces on Mindanao.

"Wendell," I said. "How the devil are you?"

"Gene, thank God you made it out of Japan."

"What are you doing here?"

"I'm in hot water with MacArthur."

"Over what?" I asked.

"It seems I exceeded my authority a bit back on Mindanao. MacArthur didn't like me calling myself *General Fertig* in the field."

"That's ridiculous," I countered. "You did what you had to do. You're a hero in your own right."

Fertig smiled. "Maybe that's why I'm in trouble."

Wendell Fertig managed to placate General MacArthur, and he and I kept in touch for many years after the war. He later headed the ROTC unit at his alma mater, the Colorado School of Mines in Golden, Colorado. After retiring, he stayed on as director of the school's alumni association.

Jim Baldwin, my friend from Zentsuji, lived in Manila, and he invited me to stay a few days with his family. During the war, Jim's mom and dad had been interned with other American civilians at Santa Thomas University. Their residence had been destroyed in battle, so they were living temporarily in a friend's enormous mansion, staffed with lots of servants and surrounded by immaculate grounds. It was unlike anything I had ever experienced.

Jim's parents were extremely wealthy in their own right and very hospitable. I stayed with them for three days and had a wonderful time. Mr. Baldwin was the president of a huge manufacturing and construction firm.

He offered me a job, which, in hindsight, I may have been foolish to turn down. But at that time I wanted to get home, visit my family, and live like an American again.*

• • •

About two weeks later my orders came through, and I knew I was going home. At that point, a large group of us left the Philippines by ship from the familiar Pier 7. The trip to America was pleasant, and after about three weeks aboard ship, I arrived at the Presidio in San Francisco on October 20, 1945. My group of veterans received an official welcome with an army band and everything. A large crowd of relatives was waiting for us, although none of my family was able to be there. That did not dampen my enthusiasm. I was home at last and could not wait to take that first step back on U.S. soil! I was so proud to be home that I knelt at the base of the gangplank and kissed the ground.

From the embarkation center in San Francisco, all former POWs were taken to an army hospital to undergo the first of a series of medical exams. The army soon put together hospital

---

* Jim headed up the company after his father retired. We corresponded regularly until Jim was killed in a yacht race in the South China Sea in 1965. I also kept up with my two friends Bob Silhavy and Clarence Madden. Madden returned to Texas after the war. But unfortunately, he passed away just a few years later. Silhavy, who moved to the Pacific Northwest and became a successful businessman, died in the early 1990s.

trains to take us to facilities closer to our homes for more in-depth treatment. In December 1945, following a stay at Schick General Hospital in Clinton, Iowa, I arrived at Borden Hospital in Chickasha, Oklahoma. Chickasha, a small town forty miles southwest of Oklahoma City, was near my official hometown of Drumright, where my mother lived. At Borden I was reunited with about thirty of my buddies from Zentsuji. Since there was nothing really wrong with me, I was released from the hospital and lodged in the Bachelor Officers' Quarters.

That stop in Chickasha was fateful, because while there I met my future wife, Betty Ruth Dietrich. Betty Ruth was a beautiful and witty twenty-two-year-old hospital employee. A POW friend named Cliff Hines introduced us. Cliff had known Betty Ruth before the war, and their parents were close. He gave me a good recommendation, which was all I needed; Betty Ruth and I hit it off from the start. She was so bright and charming that I knew right away I wanted to spend the rest of my life with her. Following a brief engagement, we were married on May 30, 1946, at the military chapel in Chickasha.

Shortly after our wedding, I applied for a discharge from the army. At first, I had hoped to stay in. But most of the officers I graduated with were now majors or lieutenant colonels. Unlike them, I had been passed over for numerous promotions because of my long stint as a POW. I felt that I had too much ground to make up to get back on the career track I wanted and decided to go civilian. I was immediately placed on administrative leave for ninety days pending the process-ing of my paperwork and given a two-week paid vacation. Betty Ruth and I used the occasion to take an extended hon-eymoon. We spent several days at a dude ranch in Texas and then bought a car and drove to California.

Things had improved tremendously in just a few months.

I was so happy, starting a new life with a young bride whom I loved very much. Now, finally, I was prepared to put the awful events of the war behind me and move on to enjoy a far better phase of my life.

• • •

On the way home from California, I applied for a job with the Bureau of Reclamation at their regional office in Boulder City, Nevada. I was tentatively offered a position at Davis Dam, Arizona, some seventy miles downstream from Boulder City. Betty Ruth and I returned to Chickasha to await my discharge from the army, which came in July 1946. Then we packed up everything and headed to Arizona. I worked as the chief of a survey party at Davis Dam, supervising structural and mechanical engineering work on the dam from 1946 to 1953, when it was completed. The immediate postwar years were the salad days of my life. Like most Americans, Betty Ruth and I experienced unprecedented prosperity. We had two sons, Robert, born in 1947, and Tom, born in 1950.

After the Davis Dam project, I continued my career with the Bureau of Reclamation, helping to construct hydro dams and powerhouses throughout the western United States. My family and I spent the next seven years at Palisades Dam in Idaho. Then I worked the following eight years at Flaming Gorge Dam in Utah, followed by another eight years on various projects in Colorado. Our lifestyle provided a terrific environment in which to raise a family. We lived in breathtaking, remote areas of the West, away from the temptations of the city. Betty Ruth, a fabulous mother, helped me teach Robert and Tom the value of hard work and righteous living. Over the years, we shared many outdoor activities, including camping, hunting, and fishing.

Before I knew it, our sons had grown up and were off to begin their own lives. Robert graduated from the University of Colorado with a degree in business and became CFO of Citibank of Nevada. He is married, has one son, Brandon, and now lives in Tulsa. Tom graduated from the U.S. Air Force Academy in 1973 and served as a captain before being medically discharged from the air force in 1976. He eventually earned a Ph.D. in marketing and is now dean of the College of Business Administration at the University of Central Oklahoma. Tom and his wife, Janice, have been married for thirty years. They have three beautiful daughters, Shoni, Kami, and Abbie.

While working in Colorado, I reached the rank of Construction Engineer in Charge of Projects. Later, I was sent to San Juan, Puerto Rico, a very different but no less idyllic location, to serve as a consultant to the Puerto Rican government for construction projects. In 1975, after my work in Puerto Rico was finished, I was able to look back with satisfaction on a rewarding and productive career in engineering. At that point, I decided to retire, and Betty Ruth and I returned to her parents' farm near Chickasha. We built our dream home on the spot where Betty Ruth grew up. We have lived there ever since and continue to enjoy life very much.

· · ·

In the spring of 1987, I was one of a handful of other Bataan survivors who returned to the Philippines to commemorate the forty-fifth anniversary of the Japanese conquest of the islands. It was strange being back after all those years. So much had changed. The capital of Manila, always a sprawling metropolis, seemed even larger and more hectic than I remembered. And I was stunned to see how the little town of Angeles had grown. The once humble village located adjacent to

Clark Field (now the enormous Clark Air Force Base) had become one of the largest cities in Asia, boasting some three million residents! While there, we ate lunch at McDonald's. I don't know who the new mayor was, but there was still no hotel called "Kingsville." I checked.

Angeles symbolized the spirit and optimism of the modern Philippines. But we had come to revisit the hallowed ground of its war-torn past. Our journey of remembrance took us to places we could never forget, the sights of so much suffering long ago. At Manila, I finally did what I had decided against on the morning of April 9, 1942. I hopped a boat for Corregidor. Walking ashore was like stepping back in time. "The Rock" looked just as it had in 1942. Bomb craters marred the once mighty fortress, and much of the island had literally been blown into the sea. Standing amid the fortress ruins, I felt closer to the ghosts of Bataan than at any time since the war's end.

Back on Luzon, my group revisited the locations where the Japanese had held us captive. The spot on which Camp O'Donnell had been located was just a big desolate field. Nothing from the old prison remained. I was dismayed that not even a historic marker identified the spot of such death and anguish. Fortunately, the situation was different at Cabanatuan. There, a large and impressive memorial honored the camp's victims.

At Capas I found a museum dedicated to preserving the history and artifacts of the Death March. The exhibit featured one of the wooden railcars that POWs were herded into for transport from San Fernando. Although much older and weathered now, it still looked uncomfortably familiar.

On May 6 we attended a lovely ceremony at the National War Monument in Manila. May 6, the date in 1942 that Corregidor fell and the Japanese gained complete control of the islands, is a national holiday in the Philippines. The Filipinos celebrate it the way we celebrate Memorial Day. Many people from all over the world were there, including several foreign dignitaries. I even got to meet S. Laurel, the vice president (and later president) of the Philippines. He was a pleasant and gracious man. I noted with satisfaction that the Japanese ambassador to the Philippines had come. This was an appropriate gesture, a small but important way to acknowledge the pain his government had inflicted on so many of us all those years ago. In tribute, a military band played the national anthems of all the Allied nations that had helped free the Philippines from Japanese tyranny. Their flags were also displayed with much pomp and pageantry. But it was the ordinary Filipinos who really made me feel gratified. So many people greeted me warmly and expressed sincere appreciation for what America did on their behalf. It felt good, if a bit awkward, to be held in such high regard.

The most emotional moment of the trip occurred just north of Mariveles, when the other survivors and I retraced some of our steps along the Death March. It was a strange experience; everything was at once very different but the same. The road was now paved, and the jungle on both sides had been cleared for expansive farmland. Yet, the aura of the place was unmistakable. My memories of the march, such as the heat, the sickness, the fear, and the physical agony, were painfully vivid. But they did not distract me from remembering those who died there. Afterward, I left the Philippines satisfied that I had done all I could to honor their supreme sacrifice.

It was definitely a bittersweet trip, but one I am very glad to have made.

EPILOGUE

WHY?

It is the ultimate mark of success when a person can look back on his days and smile at a life well lived. At age eighty-six, I am proud to say that, all and all, mine has been a life well spent. I was blessed with a great mother who instilled in me a healthy desire to succeed. I have had the best family a man could wish for.

Through good times and bad, I have remained true to my core convictions. They include the importance of hard work, self-reliance, optimism, and the sacred bond of family. I have imparted these values to my children and grandchildren, as well. I hope that today's parents will do the same for their kids; such ideals are critical for sustaining a strong, decent society in the years to come.

I feel privileged to have been a young man during the defining moments of the modern age and to have fought for freedom and justice in history's greatest war. The significance of the Battle of Bataan cannot be overestimated, and I take great pride in my service there.

By holding out until April 1942, we delayed the Japanese long enough for the Allies to marshal the forces needed to halt their advance in the Pacific and to save Australia. Bataan also served as a rallying point for the rest of the country. Spurred to action by the atrocities we endured, America regrouped, fought back, and ultimately won the war.

In recalling the sacrifices made at Bataan, I hope that people also remember the Filipino citizen-soldiers who fought and died there. Like us Americans, they did their best to preserve liberty in their homeland. I especially thank those ordinary civilians who risked their lives to give the prisoners water and sugar cane during the Death March. They probably saved thousands—including me. I doubt there are any monuments to those anonymous Samaritans, but there should be, because they did simple yet noble things for the POWs.

I want to make one thing clear about my wartime service. I am *not* a hero. I saw real heroes in action, however—men such as Tom Griffin, who saved my life during the Death March; Dr. Van Peenen, the physician who did so much with so little at Zentsuji; and Major Orr, who risked his life in support of prisoners' rights in Japan. These fine men, and countless others like them, deserve our adoration for their bravery and self-sacrifice. Without officers of their caliber, we could not have defeated the Japanese.

I, on the other hand, am merely a *survivor* of Bataan and the prison camps. My savvy and will to live carried me through some tight scrapes. I was also lucky not to be killed on a whim by mindless guards or to fall victim to the rampant disease that claimed the lives of so many POWs. In doing what I had to do to get by, I suffered humiliating abuse and deprivation. Over the years people have told me that they never would have been able to swallow their dignity as I and the other survivors did. They claim that the first time a Japanese soldier slapped them, the fight would have been on. But that is foolish talk, the kind of stupid bravado that got people bayoneted. I learned early in the Death March that *any* resistance meant certain death. Since I wanted to live, I did as ordered, just as any sane person would do. I hated every minute of it, and I hope that no American ever has to go through anything like that again. But if there is one indelible lesson that Bataan taught me, it is to be grateful for every good thing I have. In my own quiet way, I thank God daily for the blessings of peace, prosperity, and love.

· · ·

As the population of the Greatest Generation dwindles each day, the allure of World War II history is becoming stronger. More people than ever are searching for information about the war. I only hope they will find the truth. Unfortunately, in this age of political correctness, many historians have chosen to bolster the image of non-Western groups such as the Japanese, even if they have to "reinterpret" history to do it. I have seen this happen more and more in recent years, particularly with respect to the attack on Pearl Harbor. Occasionally now, the Japanese are portrayed as victims of American imperialism who had no choice but to fight to preserve their culture and way of life. In reality, the Japanese were as aggressive in the Pacific as their allies, the Nazis, were in Europe. How often do you hear the Nazis referred to as *victims*?

This truth-be-damned approach to history is a dangerous trend. For any record of the past to be meaningful, it must be accurate. That concern was a powerful incentive for me to write this book. As I stated in the Introduction, I hope my personal account will help legitimate historians assemble a comprehensive picture of World War II in the Pacific. Many other veterans have also written about Bataan, and I encourage you to read their work as well. When seeking to understand such a complex event, diligent study is necessary to get the whole story.

Let me close by addressing a question I am asked frequently when discussing my days as a POW. Ever since the counterculture revolution of the 1960s and the military embarrassment of Vietnam, people have wondered whether today's "spoiled and pampered" youngsters possess the mettle to fight and win a war the way we did. Certainly, it is hard for teens today. They face temptations and pressures that I never dealt with, and it seems many of them lack self–discipline and respect for others. But I refuse to believe that the majority of our youth are in any kind of decline. I am proud of the military service of my sons. Robert enlisted in the U.S. Navy, serving in Japan as a hospital corpsman from 1970 to 1974. Tom was a cadet at the U.S. Air Force Academy from 1969 to 1973.

Most of today's youngsters will grow to be decent and productive adults. One day, they will be tested in war, just as my generation was long ago. Many of them will suffer greatly at the hands of their enemies. But they, too, will persevere, and the country will be stronger in the end. That is powerful testimony to the enduring greatness of the American people.

• • •

I am often asked why the Japanese treated the Americans so terribly on the Death March. After more than sixty years of contemplation, I have identified six factors that best explain it for me.

The first involves the widespread acceptance of physical abuse within the Imperial Army itself. Battery was seen as a legitimate tool for toughening recruits for combat. Having a high pain threshold became a badge of strength in the Japanese military, the trademark of a rugged soldier. On Bataan I repeatedly saw Japanese enlisted men slapped and beaten for seemingly no reason. Their most punishing, hands-on commanders were noncommissioned officers such as sergeants, who often knocked privates to the ground. If a soldier did not get up immediately and stand at rigid attention, the noncommissioned officer continued to beat him unmercifully until he did. Afterward, both men would walk away as if nothing out of the ordinary had transpired. When the Japanese treated their own men so badly, it is not surprising that they abused and murdered enemy captives. The commissioned officers, such as captains and majors, seemed to enjoy seeing death. Usually, when prisoners were killed, a commissioned officer gave the command, then stood back and watched as a sergeant carried it out. Such a mindset made it easy for their soldiers to treat us harshly.

The strict regimentation of Japanese military life was the second factor. Complete obedience was demanded of subordinates, even if instructed to carry out suicide attacks. That mentality, influenced by the ancient samurai tradition, instilled in their men a willingness to follow orders unquestioningly. It allowed the Japanese to create a fighting force that exhibited no compassion toward prisoners, one capable of perpetrating the hideous acts I witnessed on the Death March.

A third factor centers on the caliber of men involved. The soldiers assigned to escort us on the Death March were the worst in the Japanese attack force. The best fighters were sent to assault Corregidor or to secure defensive positions. Our Japanese guards were inglorious "baby sitters" in their glory-bound hierarchy. That shamed them in the eyes of their peers. They angrily blamed POWs for the disgrace and therefore had it in for us. Most of the guards were youngsters, eager to prove their worth to the higher-ups. They did horrible things, often just to impress a comrade who was looking on. The guards also wanted to demonstrate their ferocity. The best way to do that was to brutalize their captives.

The status of Corregidor presented a fourth problem for the American and Filipino prisoners. The Japanese high command was furious because, when General King surrendered Bataan on April 9, the order did not include the coveted stronghold at the mouth of Manila Bay. When I began the Death March, General Wainwright was still firmly dug in on Corregidor. Because of this situation, the Japanese were not feeling at all benevolent toward us.

The timetable for the march was a fifth factor working against us. The Japanese had orders to move prisoners out of Bataan quickly, but they did not realize what bad shape we were in. We could not hike the long distances they expected us to without adequate food, water, and rest. The guards interpreted this as a sign of the inherent weakness of Americans, not the after-effects of a long siege. We POWs were the only Yankees most of them had ever seen, and they formed a stereotypical view of Americans as being cowardly, based on our unrepresentative image. To an army that valued strength above all else, those characteristics further diminished our worth in their eyes. Also, the fact that we surrendered, rather than fighting to the death as the Japanese would have done, only made us more undeserving of respect.

The final factor contributing to our mistreatment stemmed from a desire for retribution for the crucial battlefield delays that I alluded to earlier. In early 1942, at the height of its prowess, the Japanese high command promised to glorify Emperor Hirohito by taking the Philippines in a month. At the time, it must have seemed like an easy pledge to keep. The Americans were outnumbered; our air force was destroyed; our supply lines were cut off; and we were defending the islands with antiquated weaponry. The Japanese did not anticipate our will to resist or our adaptability under fire. Instead, it took them *four* months to conquer the Philippines. This was an embarrassing failure that the enemy found hard to swallow. Their honor tarnished, they were hell-bent on punishing us for offering such protracted and costly opposition.

I want to reiterate that in no way do my theories excuse the actions of the Japanese guards during the Death March. Whatever they thought of Americans or the emperor's "glorious" war ambitions, the fact is that those men systematically beat, starved, and murdered thousands of defenseless POWs. In my opinion, they are among the most notorious war criminals of all time and should always be regarded as such.

AFTERWORD

Gene Boyt died on Patriot Day, September 11, 2003. He is remembered as a decent, honest man who lived a remarkable life. His family and friends miss him dearly; yet they take comfort in knowing that he has answered reveille in a far better place.

SOURCES

The works listed below provided historical background.

Miller, E. F. *Bataan Uncensored.* Long Prairie, Minn.: Hart Publications, Inc., 1949; 2d ed., Military Historical Society of Minnesota, 1991.

Olson, John E. *O'Donnell: Andersonville of the Pacific.* Carlisle Barracks, Pa.: U.S. Army Military History Institute, 1985.

Sides, Hampton. *Ghost Soldiers: The Forgotten Epic Story of World War II's Most Dramatic Mission.* New York: Random House, 2001.

Sulzberger, C. L. *The American Heritage Picture History of World War II.* New York: American Heritage Pub. Co., 1966.

Tenney, Lester. *My Hitch in Hell: The Bataan Death March.* Washington, D.C.: Brassey's, 1995.

INDEX

O'Donnell, Camp,
141–42, 144–50, 152,
155–57, 161, 197, 216
Officers' Row, 38
Okayama, Japan, 195–96
Okinawa, Japan, 201
Oklahoma (U.S.S.), 54
Oklahoma City, 112, 213
Olson, Maj. John, 111
Orr, Maj. William,
167–68, 172–73, 204,
220
Osaka, Japan, 164, 172,
177, 196, 199

P-35s (fighter planes), 59
P-38s (fighter planes), 209
P-40s (fighter planes), 59,
81
POW(s), 125–26, 130–32,
135, 139, 150, 164–65, 167,
171–72, 174, 177, 183, 189,
191–93, 195, 198, 201–202,
205–206, 210, 213, 216,
220–22, 224–25
Pacific, 33, 73, 133, 163,
220–222
Pacific Command, 78
Palisades Dam (Idaho),
214
Pearl Harbor, Hawaii, 34,
50, 53–54, 81, 221

Phemister, J. W., Dr.
(maternal grandfather),
3–5, 11
Phemister, Julia (maternal
grandmother), 4
Philippine Army, 73
Philippine Campaign, 27
Philippine Scouts, 113
Philippines, 29–31, 33–35,
37–39, 41, 43, 45–48, 50,
62, 69, 73, 79, 81, 83, 123,
136, 142, 164, 168, 197,
204, 212, 215–17, 225
Pier 7, 157, 212
Ponca City, Okla., Boyt's
early life in, 8
Powell, Robert, 190
President Cleveland, SS, 32,
34–35, 114, 136
Presidio, the, 32, 212

Quartermaster Corps,
6n, 69

Rackmill, Lt. Larry,
148–51, 153–54
Rangers, 205–206
Red Cross, 189–92, 205,
207
Red Feather Lakes, 18–19
Remsnyder, Lt. Warren,
112

United States Corps of Engineers (USCE), 31

U.S. Air Force Academy, 215, 222

U.S. Army, 25, 47, 67–68, 72, 81, 116, 141; Far East Command, 36; U.S. Eighth Army, 206

U.S. Cavalry, 25–26

U.S. Embassy in Tokyo, 185

U.S. Navy, 183, 222

Van Peenen, Dr., 183–84, 220

Vitamin B1, 168–69

Vitamin C, 170

Wainwright, Gen. Jonathan, 63, 81, 224

Wake Island, 48

War Department, 65, 71n

Washington, D.C., 36, 65

World War I, 6–7, 22, 31, 36, 67

World War II, 28, 221–22

Yokohama Harbor, 209

Yokohama, Japan, 206

Zamboanga, Philippines, 47

Zentsuji, Camp, 177–81, 184–86, 190–91, 193, 195, 211, 213, 220

Zero fighters (zeros), 58–59, 74–75

Zero Ward, 147

Zigzag trenches, 64